T0344344

BBQ

A PARTY

BBQ

PETER DE CLERCQ

A PARTY

LANNOO

CONTENTS

3 FISH DISHES

4 MEAT DISHES

CONTENTS

> INTRODUCTION

A life of fire

As a twelve-year-old boy I dreamt of becoming a butcher. My father's brother was a butcher and it appealed to me. I soon decided to head to the *Ter Groene Poorte* butchery school in Bruges in order to learn the trade. It kept me busy and I also took on a weekend job with my uncle, taking the train every Friday to Knokke-Heist. My main job was to help with the barbecue and I learned a great deal from the foreman, Hans Stul, who today has a fantastic butchery in Kortemark. Slowly I learned about the pleasures of the kitchen and after completing my training as butcher I went on to train as a chef at *Ter Groene Poorte*.

I graduated at the age of eighteen, around the same time that I met my wife, Annouk. When I was first invited over by my father-in-law, Alex van Landschoot – yes, something of a name in the meat industry – to my great disbelief he stood there grilling a full rack of beef ribs in the fireplace. He was also obsessed with barbecuing and I was allowed to help him on weekends. Often we organized barbecue parties for the entire family. After my national service, when I was twenty, we both decided to convert part of his house and make it into a restaurant and grill serving T-bone steaks and shrimp. That is how *Elckerlijc* came about in 1990. The name refers to the 15th century morality play 'Everyman', and everyone *is* welcome in our restaurant. We primarily wanted to create an accessible restaurant. It didn't stop at shrimp; gradually we went after a certain refinement and added duck breast or lamb brochette. In 1996 we got the chance to buy *Elckerlijc* from my

father-in-law. Suddenly I became my own boss and was able to give my creativity free reign. I opted to cook everything on the barbecue and worked hard at learning all possible techniques. Back then very little was known about barbecues and there were no books on the subject. Slowly but surely, customers began to ask me more about it all, for example, about how to prepare sole or quail on the barbecue. I began to write everything down and eventually it became my first cookbook, *Eigentijds barbecuen* (The Modern BBQ). It was the first Dutch language book about barbecuing on the market. And it was a real hit, as nothing had yet been written on the subject. The media picked up on the book and I was offered my own barbecue program on regional TV, *Pottenkijker*. Along with the Belgian Barbecue federation, I entered the World BBQ Championship in 2001. We didn't win, but we learned a lot from the experience. Two years later we entered the competition again, this time with a new team that was better prepared. That time, in Jamaica, we walked away with the world championship title.

For me, that was the inspiration I needed to find out even more about the world of barbecuing; to study it across the entire world and broaden my own horizons. For example, in Argentina I took

Locally grown

organic

part in a variety of *asados* or barbecues. On one occasion I had to cook a huge rump of veal on an open barbecue in the middle of an open field. Normally I would have used a closed barbecue for something like that so that the meat could cook slowly and evenly from the inside and to give it a lovely, brown crust on the outside. So I made a sort of natural *papillote* from the long wet grass and shaped it around the meat to cook it for three to four hours. As a result, I discovered that it not only ensured proper cooking, but also gave the meat a delicious aroma. I had another such useful experience in Laos where, every few yards, the people in local markets stood barbecuing fresh fish from the Mekong River. They would spear them on something like a piece of bamboo and that gave me the idea to experiment with various types of wood, as they give a particular flavor to the meat. It's often by chance that you come across a new technique or flavor and so I took a piece of tree bark from the garden to use on the barbecue, but the outer shell fell off. I wondered if the meat wouldn't grill on it, so I soaked the piece of wood in water for some weeks and then used it as a shell, with the delicious woody taste that it gave to the meat.

BBQ as a cooking method

I am a dedicated barbecuer, opting to barbecue as often as possible. The grill lends so many flavors and helps to bring out the best in authentic products. The fact that it's a noble technique has fully come to light over the past few years, with increasing numbers of restaurants having one or more grill dishes on their menus.

BBQ can be sophisticated

People are immersed in cooking shows these days; something that I encourage. I think it's particularly due to the fact that they're inspired to be a little more sophisticated in their cooking at home. We eat with our mouths and with our noses, but we also enjoy how our food looks, and you yourself know that if something looks delicious, it also tastes a great deal better.

Barbecue dishes are generally served in a pretty straightforward way: big pieces of meat on a plate and a side dish that you can serve yourself from a buffet. In this book I'd like to show you that it's possible to do something a little different. Barbecuing lends itself just as well to the presentation of fresh, modern food and you'll see that a little extra effort really is worth it and that guests will feel incredibly spoiled. Be inspired by the photography in this book and turn your barbecue into both a culinary treat and a sophisticated party.

Barbecue: fresh and pure

Barbecuing is about the authentic product and it should be an experience from start to finish. That is why it's vital to work with fresh, natural ingredients. The crackling fire, cooking outdoors and working with quality meat, fish and homegrown vegetables brings out the caveman in us all. I get my love of fresh vegetables from my grandparents who had a huge vegetable garden. Over the last few years I have discovered how easy it is to grow your own vegetables, fruits and herbs and that is why we set up our own garden for our restaurant: Elckerlijc Farm. It's fantastic to see how a young leek grows and how the end result winds up on your plate. It gives a real sense of satisfaction.

We also raise our own pigs on a neighboring farm; we feed them only steamed potatoes, grain wash, whey, corn and supplementary feed. It gives them a unique, delicate taste and keeps the meat moist and juicy. The pigs are butchered at the *G. van Landschoot & Sons* slaughterhouse, an expanding and increasingly innovative business. They have a strict policy of animal-friendly treatment and the infrastructure is completely modernized. There are new pigpens with under-floor heating, ventilation and a gentle sprinkler system so that the animals experience as little stress as possible. This also guarantees the superior quality of the meat.

Pork has recently undergone something of a renaissance in popularity; no longer seen, as it once was, as a less desirable kind of meat. Another positive step is that an increasing number of butchers and shops are opting for grass-fed beef. It produces meat with much more flavor. I know that most people opt for lean meat, but believe me, there is so much more flavor and aroma in well-marbled meat. Along some of the smaller roads you often see local farmers advertising their own fruit and vegetables. If you get the chance, stop off at these places to do your shopping. Think carefully about where you buy your products when organizing a barbecue, working with pure and natural products is very important.

BARBECUE: THE BASIS

Charcoal or gas?

It remains a real issue for many people: should you go for the traditional charcoal barbecue or can you also use a gas one? Personally, I don't find selecting a proper barbecue easy, even though I work with them on a daily basis. Charcoal brings you in contact with real fire, with the scents and the distinctive smell of smoke. But with wood chips and other aromatics, you can create the same effect on a gas barbecue. Personally, I prefer a wood fire. But don't get distracted by the huge range of barbecues on offer, just choose a safe and user-friendly one. Anyone can do this: all you need is a bundle of newspapers, a match and charcoal or briquettes. I have a slight preference for coconut-shell briquettes: they give a lovely, more steady heat than charcoal and they burn longer, which means that you don't have to use as much and they blaze up less when hit by drips from the meat or juice pan.

Open or closed?

If you are planning to buy a new barbecue then this might be the right moment to go for a closed barbecue. It holds the heat better and is more constant so that the aromas are more easily spread; it's ideal for grilling larger pieces of meat. Plus, you can always use this kind of barbecue with the lid off. Throughout the recipes that follow, you will notice that I often make suggestions about extra aromatic herbs that you can throw on the fire: either herbs for the fire, olive pits or fresh pine needles. Grape vine prunings, wood shavings infused with Jack Daniels or simple dried herbs can be a real treat for the nose. Don't forget from time to time to add some additional aromatic wood shavings, olive pits or herbs to the fire.

Making fire

The art of a good barbecue is to make sure that you don't end up with a huge fire: it will only burn the food. Wait until you have a lovely, glowing, gray heap of coals, covered by a thick layer of gray or white ash. I don't care for chemical fire starters, but prefer the natural variations with paraffin. You can use a starter tube to light your charcoal or coconut briquettes. It's a straight tube perforated with air holes underneath. You can use it to heat up to 5.5 lbs (2.5 kg) of briquettes, which will be enough to barbecue for three to four hours. It will be ready in about twenty minutes, allowing you to enjoy a drink beforehand. You can regulate the temperature of the barbecue via the air vent underneath: high temperatures are achieved by opening the air vent, lower ones by closing it. Closing the top and bottom air vents will make the fire go out.

With a gas barbecue, the burner and the flames must be far enough away from the grill (at least 4 in / 10 cm). You'll be able to work best with a grill over a flame to which you can add some herbs for the fire or other aromatics.

A few essential tips

› Make sure there is a 'cool' zone in the barbecue where there is almost no charcoal. If the meat starts to cook too quickly, you can place it over that section to cool it down and to make sure that it cooks slower. This method is called indirect barbecuing and is a good way to keep food from burning.

› Always wipe the grill with a little grease or oil beforehand to prevent food from sticking. Clean the grill with a steel brush while it's still warm. This will make clean-up much easier. You could also give it a quick clean by wiping it with half a lemon or a slice of pineapple.

- Always make sure that pork and chicken are thoroughly cooked. Frozen fish and meat can be put on the barbecue, but must have been professionally frozen which means frozen with nitrogen. It ensures that the meat is frozen instantly, whereas home freezing is a slow process and the ice crystals get into the tissue of the meat and damage it. Always make sure that you allow frozen meat or fish to defrost solely in the refrigerator. Fresh meat or fresh fish are best kept for as long as possible in the refrigerator or cooler.

- White meats require more herbs than red meats.

- Firm types of fish (monkfish, salmon and tuna) can easily be put onto skewers. Less firm fish such as cod can best be cooked in a fish grill.

- Don't forget about what's available in your own garden. Experiment with the wood from your fruit trees. You'll be surprised at the variety of tastes and aromas that can be created.

- Make a 'bath' of wine, stock or beer in a fireproof bowl. Placing this in a closed barbecue releases all kinds of delicious aromas and will keep meat juicy and moist.

Don't forget

You don't need much to get started barbecuing, but there are a few things you can't do without:

- Stainless-steel tongs: you can use these to turn food without burning your hands.
- A meat fork: makes it easy to quickly place food on the grill. Make sure that you don't pierce the meat once it's seared to seal in the flavor.
- A brush: I always brush ingredients with a marinade or basic oil. There are a number of suggestions in this book and the advantage of this extra layer is that your meat or fish will brown more evenly.
- A fish grill: a grill with a non-stick layer in which you can place more delicate ingredients such as fish so they won't fall apart.
- A good knife and cutting board.
- A barbecue apron.
- A bucket of water for washing your hands.

Safety first

- Put a plant spray bottle full of water next to the barbecue in the event that any flames shoot out. Keep a bucket of sand close by so that you can quickly extinguish any small fires.
- Small flames can also be put out by throwing a handful of salt over the coals.

- Place the barbecue on a stable foundation and choose a solid, high-quality barbecue.
- Never try to move a burning barbecue.
- Soak wooden skewers and chips in water overnight before using them.
- Make sure you have an oven mitt available; it should come up above the elbow, but allow you to feel what you're doing.

Special barbecues

In this book we indicate the type of barbecue that best suits every recipe. This does not mean that there are no alternatives: you can make pretty much anything on a closed barbecue; it's only for things like pizza, for example, that you might need a tool such as a pizza stone.

Le Panyol

This oven is constructed from firebricks, a unique fired clay stone from the white earth of Larnage. The natural warmth of the wood fire is quickly stored by the firebricks, which can reach a temperature of 752 °F / 400 °C in less than an hour. When the ash is removed, the oven remains warm for quite some time. As well as pizzas and bread, you can also cook meat or fish on its base.

Green Egg

The Big Green Egg has its origins in East Asia. This kind of oven was developed some three thousand years ago in China. The Japanese took over the principle of the oven and called it a *kamado* (oven, fireplace). After the Second World War, the *kamado* was discovered by the Americans, who brought it back from Japan. 1974 saw the introduction of the very first Big Green Egg: not made of breakable clay, but from space-age ceramics. This material, developed by NASA, is exceptionally durable and is resistant to even the most extreme temperatures. Real barbecue lovers soon discovered this unique bit of equipment and the international advance of the Big Green Egg became unstoppable. The Green Egg is suitable for baking, frying, grilling and smoking. The ceramic housing ensures optimal control and an even distribution of heat.

Grill Dome

This American company has been developing and producing ceramic barbecues for some twenty years. It's less well known than the Big Green Egg, but works on the same principle.

The fireplace

You don't need all kinds of expensive barbecues to be able to cook. Anyone with a fireplace can easily use it for grilling. For most people this is a bridge too far, which is a shame because the possibilities are endless. For example, you could hang a cast-iron pan over the fire for delicious winter stews. Throwing a few herbs onto the fire will create a fantastic aromatic barbecue atmosphere. And anyone who is any good at DIY could quickly build a grill to put over the fire. You would only need to throw on some coals, shove some burning pieces of wood to the back and you could start cooking. These days there are all kinds of handy grills available for fireplaces.

Green Egg

Le Panyol

Smoking for beginners

If you would like to try smoking something on the barbecue, then it's a good idea to use a barbecue with a lid. Smoking is an indirect thing: when using a charcoal fire, you divide the charcoal into two heaps on each side; with a gas barbecue you only use the outer burners. This helps to create a colder zone underneath the fish, allowing it to cook slower and letting the smoky aromas do their work. Smoking with the help of a smoking chamber or smoke oven is called hot smoking. During the process, the food is partly steamed. A smoking chamber or smoke oven for a gas barbecue consists of a sort of roaster with a tight-fitting lid. Inside there is a grill that should be cleaned and greased before use. Under the grill there is a drip tray. You spread the smoking chips or flakes or hardwood on the bottom of the box, and this provides the smoke development. Making the woodchips wet increases the development of smoke. Every type of wood produces a different scent, giving the food its own taste and aroma. Cold smoking is done at a low temperature in smoke that is generally around 77 °F / 25 °C. The smoke enters the smoke chamber via a chimney or tube, where there is a space between the smoke chamber and the food to be smoked.

Smoking gun

You can use this piece of equipment to easily introduce smoke into things such as a glass or a glass dome. Place the wood chips or other aromatics into the top through an opening, turn on the gun and smoke is blown through the long rubber tube. It's suitable for ingredients that are otherwise difficult to smoke such as seafood or cocktails. You can opt for classic flavors such as wood chips with apple or cherry flavor, but there are also various types of tea flavors or dried flowers or herbs. Find out more at www.cuisinetechnology.com

Smoke generator

Cold smoking gives a fantastic flavor. As it says in the recipe, you can smoke things in a smoking chamber or opt for a smoke generator. Point-Virgule introduced a version created to generate smoke for up to 10 hours. The smoke generator can be used in a closed barbecue, a smoke oven or any other suitable receptacle, such as an old refrigerator or a smoking chamber. While it's called cold smoking, a small part of the generator is made up of smoldering wood chips, so bear this in mind when selecting a receptacle. For more information, see the recipe for smoked salmon with horseradish sauce on p. 91.

smoking gun

The secret of delicious beef

The secret to proper ageing

Selecting delicious, high quality meat is vital for a barbecue. I always underline the importance of properly aged meat, because it's more flavorful and succulent. One of our suppliers is the *Dierendonck Butcher* with branches in Nieuwpoort and Sint-Idesbald.

What does it mean to 'age' meat?

'Ageing' meat is something that has always been done. There are two ways of 'ageing': *dry ageing* and *wet ageing*. The wet method takes place in a vacuum-sealed plastic bag stored at a temperature of 32-34° F / 4 °C. Although the temperature can also be lower than freezing. Dry ageing takes place in a cooler in which the air is circulated. The wet method is used mainly by major industry and supermarkets as it involves as little loss in weight as possible. Dry ageing is mainly used by traditional butchers. For example, for thirty years Raymond Dierendonck, the first generation of *Dierendonck Butchers* (see photos) opted to age meat in refrigerators made of tile and concrete. The meat itself was aged on wooden racks. The combination of the concrete and the wood ensured that moisture was drawn into the meat. These refrigerators were all modernized by the second generation at Dierendonck. His son, Hendrik, who now runs the business, explains that almost no one takes the time to age meat these days:

'Ageing meat is an expensive business as it takes up a great deal of time and causes a loss of weight', explains Hendrik. 'After three weeks of ageing, there is a weight loss of 35 to 40 percent. Fatty animals are more difficult to cut and that is why the whole concept of ageing meat has been rather forgotten.'

Conditions for proper ageing

For proper ageing the butcher must meet five criteria:

› the meat must have a good layer of fat (and not be stripped of fat after being slaughtered);
› the ventilation in the cooler must be powerful enough;
› the temperature must be stable and controlled;
› the meat must be able to age for a minimum number of days;
› the cooler must have the proper level of humidity.

Every butcher meets these criteria in their own way. In America and Australia they opt for dry ageing, hanging carcasses in a refrigerator at a temperature of 39.2 °F / 0 to 2 °C with very large ventilators that ensure a good airflow. In Europe butchers tend to play more with the degree of humidity and the temperature during the various phases of ageing, which creates a more specific aged taste.

.

What does the ageing process do?

Meat that has been given time to age properly dries out somewhat, which means that the taste of the meat and the fat is heightened. The more is the meat has been aged, the stronger its taste will be and it will almost have a nutty aroma. During the ageing process the meat will also become more succulent as the natural enzymes in the meat are broken down and you will almost be able to pull the meat apart in strips. This second process can take up to three weeks for the meat to reach its maximum tenderness.

Anyone who chooses aged meat will certainly be satisfied, as this unusually delicious and high quality meat has gone through a long, careful process in order to end up on the plate.

Which kinds of meat can you age?
›   Beef: maximum of 3 months, chilled.
›   Pork: maximum of 1 week.
›   Game: up to 3 weeks.
›   Lamb: 1 to 2 weeks.
›   Mutton: 3 weeks.

Types of beef

›   **Belgian Blue**: This bodybuilder of the cattle world has a regal white coat with a touch of blue and the attitude of a bulldog.
›   **Hereford**: This breed comes from Herefordshire in the UK. They are lovely, big animals with a brown coat and a large, white head. They look as if they are wearing white coats and have short, thick legs. Sometimes they even have short horns. Well-produced Hereford meat is excellent, but is rarely sold as such; it's mostly combined with the commercial breeds and sold in supermarkets.
›   **Holstein-Friesian**: This classic black-coated milk cow is at its most delicious once the meat has been aged for three weeks.
›   **Aberdeen Angus**: A real Angus has a smooth, regal black coat. The huge bulls were once Scotland's pride, but unfortunately today there are very few pure-bred animals remaining.

›   **Charolais**: This is a commercial breed raised in the US and Australia and which enjoys warm weather. They always give good meat, but it's not of the highest quality.
›   **Dexter**: Dexters are small, peaceful animals. They are black but sometimes have a white patch on their snout. They produce very little milk, but incredibly delicious meat. Certain cuts of a properly slaughtered and aged Dexter taste sweet and smoky.
›   **Dutch Belted**: This breed of cattle is mainly recognizable from the white band between its front and hind legs around the chest and the back of an animal, the rest of which is black or red. The small to mid-sized breed of cow has strong legs. Their meat is valued due to the succulent structure and excellent flavor.
›   **Scottish Longhorn**: These powerful animals are very common along the Scottish Borders. They have long horns and a thick neck. Their coat is a lovely shade of light and dark brown. When the animal has time to graze on grass, it results in very delicious meat.
›   **Limousin**: This is perhaps the most successful breed of cattle and these days are crossed with the Angus and the Shorthorn.
›   **Scottish Highlander**: Because the Scottish Highlands are cold and wet, these cows have huge lower legs, thick flanks and a thick, red-brown wooly coat. Slaughtered at a young age they are nice looking as opposed to tasty, but once they've been allowed to roam around for four years or so, they produce good, solid, well-marbled, smoky meat.
›   **White Park**: This is one of the best breeds for meat. The animals are enormous and produce gigantic T-bones, huge ribs and incredibly tasty steaks.
›   **West Flemish Red**: The West Flemish Red is a big, tall, heavy animal bred for its milk as well as its meat.
›   **Piemontese**: This breed, originally from Italy, is famous for its peaceful nature. They are brown at birth, changing as they grow to become grey and white. They are notable for the black circles around their eyes and on the inside of their ears, their tail hair, hooves and the points of the horns.

19

› **Main-Anjou**: Originally from France's Anjou region, this largely red and white breed is bred mainly for meat production. The fibers of this meat are very fine and tender.
› **Aubrac**: This breed from Aveyron is recognizable for its red and brown color as well as the black around its eyes. The cattle are fed from May to September on the tender grass of the high moorlands of the Aubrac, at an altitude of 2,600 - 3,200 ft / 800 - 1000 m. The meat of the Aubrac is exceptionally succulent, low in fat and very rich in taste. It's a healthy, natural meat.
› **Simmental**: The Simmental are cattle originally native to the Simme and Saanen Valleys of the Swiss region of Bern. It's a local branch of the larger group of red and red skinned Mid-European valley and mountain cattle. In the eighteenth century many Simmental cattle were exported to Belgium and to Lombardy in Italy. The German Simmental from Bavaria is related to the redskins in color but has a white head. The meat has a nice covering of fat, a delicate structure and good marbling. If it comes from cows at least three years old (having calved twice) and which are very carefully raised (long growth period), the meat is incredibly tasty and sought after.
› **Chianina**: This is one of the oldest breeds of cattle; primarily known as the world's largest breed. The bulls can reach a height of 6-1/2 ft. / 2 m and weigh around 3,700 lbs / 1700 kg. Their coat is porcelain white and their skin is dark. The home of the breed is the Val di Chiana, a fertile valley near Florence. The meat contains very little cholesterol and is full of flavor. Only Chianina meat is used for the *bistecca alla Fiorentina*.

Cuts of beef

› **Fillet (tenderloin)**: This is found at the top of the rear of the back near the spine. It's the most tender and juiciest and therefore the most prized part of the cow. It's the only muscle that the animal doesn't use. The fillet is on the inside of the ribcage and fixes to the kidneys at its thinnest part. If you feel where your own kidneys are, there is a muscle that runs along the centre of the spine: this is the fillet. The fillet is surrounded by a thin layer of fat that can be easily removed with a very sharp knife and is made up of three parts. The flat end is normally used for stroganoff and steak tartare. The top is the thick section used for chateaubriand, beef wellington or as a grilling steak. The mid-section is made into tenderloin steak, tournedos and carpaccio.
› **Entrecote (Short Loin / Sirloin)**: This is the back of the cow and produces the tastiest steaks, such as the T-bone.
› **Shank**: This is found underneath the hind legs. It's a huge piece of meat that is turned into braising steak or ground beef. It's somewhat tougher, but when cut up and marinated is great for the barbecue.
› **Chuck and brisket**: These are at the front of the chest and neck. These are very active muscles, given that a healthy animal eats around 18 lbs / 8 kg of food per body weight. The meat is delicious as ground beef or for hamburgers. You can also stew the meat at a low temperature.
› **Rib (Thick rib and fore rib)**: These are behind the neck at the top; they form generally the most used muscles and therefore produce very lean, fibrous meat. When very finely sliced and marinated are very tasty on the barbecue, but also incredibly good for satay.
› **Neck**: This cut runs from the neck and along the ribs. An animal should really only be slaughtered if the neck is hanging down, as the meat will only then have the structure of good beef. The neck of a young animal has little flavor, but if taken from a cow that has been well grazed and has been able to roam free in order to build up a good weight, it can taste incredibly good. The best types of salted meat are made of this.
› **Shank**: The shanks are the same as the forearm and the lower leg in humans. The muscles are grouped around thick bones that result in delicious marrow-ripe meat. This is the absolute best for stew type dishes.
› **Oxtail**: Very different from the tenderloin is the oxtail, a gelatinous and tough piece of meat around the bones that form the tail. You can stew this for a few hours to prepare it and you can also use it to make a delicious sauce.

1
THE BASICS

> THE BASICS

A. Oil

Rosemary oil
Take eight sprigs of rosemary. Cook them briefly in a closed barbecue. Put them into a 1 quart / 1 liter bottle and pour lukewarm olive oil over them. Leave it to infuse for six weeks.

 Delicious with grilled lamb.

Lemon oil
Wash ten lemons – preferably organic – in hot water. Cut them into quarters and place them into a glass jar. Add a few sprigs of fresh thyme and some bay leaves and cover it all in hot olive oil at 170 °F / 75 °C. Leave to infuse for six weeks.

 Delicious with grilled T-bone.

B. Herbs

Herbs for vegetables
1-1/2 Tbs / 20 g coriander seeds
1 Tbs / 15 g cumin seeds
1 tsp / 5 g mustard seeds
1-1/2 tsp / 8 g peppercorns

Toast the herbs in a steel skillet and grind the mixture in a coffee grinder or mixer. Then combine this with:

½ tsp / 2 g ground ginger
1 tsp / 4 g turmeric powder
½ tsp / 2 g curry powder
1/8 tsp / 1 g mace
2 tsp / 10 g sea salt

Herbs for fish
1-3/4 cups / 500 g sea salt
½ cup / 50 g dill
¼ cup / 25 g fennel
¼ cup / 25 g parsley
2 Tbs / 25 g paprika
1 Tbs / 12 g cayenne pepper
1 Tbs / 12 g curry powder

Herbs for grilling
coriander seeds
juniper berries
thyme
rosemary
bay leaf
oregano

Herbs for meat
1-3/4 cups / 500 g sea salt
2 Tbs / 25 g basil
2 Tbs / 25 g thyme
2 Tbs / 25 g rosemary
2 Tbs / 25 g oregano
2 Tbs / 25 g black pepper

Herbs for the barbecue
1-1/2 Tbs / 20 g sea salt
2 tsp / 10 g cayenne pepper
1-1/2 Tbs / 20 g paprika
2 tsp / 10 g curry powder
1 tsp / 5 g basil
1 tsp / 5 g thyme

C. Marinades

Combine all of the ingredients for a marinade and allow the mixture to infuse for while. The marinade can be stored for a long time and will become more concentrated over time.

Meat marinade
2 cups / 0.5 liters grill oil
1 cup / 2.5 dl basil oil
1 cup / 2.5 dl Italian herb oil
1/3 cup / 1 dl walnut oil
1-1/2 Tbs / 20 g dried basil
1-1/2 Tbs / 20 g coriander seeds
1-1/2 Tbs / 20 g black peppercorns
1-1/2 Tbs / 20 g dried rosemary
6 chili peppers
10 cloves of garlic, whole
4 sprigs of dried thyme
4 bay leaves

Fish marinade
2 cups / 0.5 liters grill oil
1 cup / 2.5 dl garlic and fine herb oil
1 cup / 2.5 dl basil oil
1-1/2 Tbs / 20 g fennel seeds

6 cloves of garlic, whole
4 bay leaves
4 sprigs of lemon thyme
2 tsp / 10 g curry powder
2 tsp / 10 g oregano

D. Basting marinades

Basting marinades can be used to quickly and easily give flavor to large pieces of meat or fish. For example, with a chicken you would baste the marinade in-between the skin and the meat. It produces a much juicier chicken with a lovely color. With a thick piece of cod you can baste a green marinade in-between the layers of the fish to give it a nicely marbled structure. You can also do this with fruit: for example, baste a pineapple with a delicious mint coulis and place the whole thing on the barbecue.

Chinese marinade
8 tsps of honey
5 cloves of garlic
¾ in / 2 cm ginger
7/8 cup / 2 dl soy sauce
1/3 cup / 1 dl rice vinegar
4 tsps of dry sherry
1/2 tsp of Chinese five spice powder
1/2 tsp of sea salt
1/2 tsp of ground black pepper

Warm the honey in a stainless-steel pan, crush the garlic and grate the ginger into the pan. Deglaze with the soy sauce, rice vinegar and sherry. Add the Chinese five spice powder, salt and pepper. Strain it through a piece of muslin and store it in a sealed jar in the refrigerator.

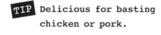 **TIP** Delicious for basting chicken or pork.

Dark beer marinade

1 can of Gordon Finest Scotch
2 bay leaves
2 tsps of brown sugar
2 sprigs of thyme
2 tsps of cardamom pods
2 tsps of mixed spice
2 tsps of sea salt
1 fresh red chili, finely chopped

Place everything into a stainless-steel pan. Bring it to a boil and then allow the mixture to cool completely. Strain it through a piece of muslin and store in a sealed jar in the refrigerator.

 Delicious with leg of lamb, pork and chicken.

Blonde beer marinade

1 orange, preferably organic
2 cloves of garlic
1 bottle of blonde bourgogne des flandres beer
2 cloves
2 tsps of coriander seeds
1 bay leaf
1 cinnamon stick
2 tsps of sea salt
2 tsps of black peppercorns

Cut the orange into pieces leaving the rind on. Crush the cloves of garlic. Place all of the ingredients into a stainless-steel pan. Bring them to a boil and then remove from the heat. Once the mixture has cooled completely, strain through a piece of muslin. Store in a sealed jar in the refrigerator.

 Delicious with leg of lamb, pork and chicken.

Green herb marinade

1/3 cup / 1 dl white wine
1/3 cup / 1 dl sake
juice of 1 lemon
2 tsps of sea salt
4 tsps of black peppercorns
4 tsps of fresh tarragon leaves
4 tsps of fresh basil
2 tsps of fresh dill
2 tsps of fresh coriander leaves (cilantro)

Bring the white wine, sake and the lemon juice to a boil with the salt and the peppercorns. Then add the fresh herbs and mix. Allow it to cool, strain through muslin and store in a sealed jar in the refrigerator.

 Delicious with all types of fish.

Red wine marinade

1-1/2 cups / 3.5 dl red wine
7/8 cup / 2 dl water
2 sprigs of thyme
2 sprigs of rosemary
2 tsps of sea salt
1/3 cup / 1 dl Worcestershire sauce
3 cloves of garlic, crushed
1/3 cup / 1 dl soy sauce

Bring everything to a boil and then leave to cool. Strain through muslin and store in a sealed jar in the refrigerator.

Peanut marinade
2 cups / 50 cl olive oil
2/3 cup / 150 g peanut butter
2 tsps of tomato puree
1 cup / 2.5 dl coconut milk
2 cloves of garlic, crushed
2 tsps of salt
1/3 cup / 100 g honey
1 tsp ground ginger
1 tsp ground cumin
1/3 cup / 1 dl water

Heat everything together and leave it to cool before straining through a piece of muslin. Store in a sealed jar in the refrigerator.

Timmermans cherry beer and mint marinade
2/3 cup / 200 g honey
1 cinnamon stick
2 star anise
4 cardamom pods
1/3 cup / 1 dl water
2 cups / 5 dl Timmermans cherry beer
1 bunch of fresh mint

Heat the honey with the herbs and deglaze with the water and the cherry beer. Allow to cool and add the mint. Strain the mixture through a fine sieve. Store in a sealed jar in the refrigerator.

 TIP Prick a few holes in the bottom of a pineapple and inject with this marinade. Place the pineapple on the barbecue for 1 hour, then slice it up and serve with a scoop of ice-cream.

E. Herb stock and fish fumet

Herb stock
4 white celery stalks
3 large carrots
5 onions
thyme and bay leaf, preferably fresh
4 tsps of black peppercorns
1 tsp / 30 g cayenne pepper
1 chili
5 quarts / 5 liters of water

Wash the vegetables and cut them into large pieces. Cook the vegetables with the herbs in the water for 20 minutes.

Fish fumet

Use the same ingredients and follow the same method as for the herb stock, but then without the cayenne pepper and the chili and with 3.33 lbs / 1.5 kg heads and bones of firm, lean white fish (turbot, plaice, dab, red gurnard, cod, halibut or brill). The fish gills and eyes must always be removed.

PARTY FORMULA

> 1 <

A smooth cocktail party

There's nothing better than a delicious cocktail on a swinging summer's day. Cocktails create an instant party atmosphere and make you feel as if you're on vacation. Throw in a barbecue and the party can't fail. Serve a few snacks from this book or make up a mixture of delicious fish, meat or veggie dishes.

Below are a few of the most delicious cocktail dishes that came about through our collaboration with the Belgian Barflies, a collective of three young, talented men who lost their hearts to these fashionable drinks. I met them and, after a few animated conversations, we decided that the two worlds – that of barbecuing and cocktails making – are closer together than we could have imagined. Certain barbecue techniques, for example, go perfectly with creating cocktails: a drink with a smoky taste creates an extra effect for the nose and the taste buds! The Belgian Barflies discovered new ideas as a result of this meeting and together we developed a series of fashionable cocktails designed for barbecuing.

Cocktail ABC

Stir/Shake: Why does James Bond always ask for a martini *shaken, not stirred*, while a martini should be *stirred, not shaken*? *Stirring* or mixing a cocktail with a bar spoon is suitable for mixing all pure alcoholic drinks such as a martini (gin and vermouth or vodka). *Shaking* would 'bruise' the alcohol too much. Stirring is a more subtle, softer way of mixing cocktails, while shaking is for fruit juice based cocktails, or those with cream or egg white bases. According to Ian Fleming's biographer Andrew Lycett, the writer preferred his martini to be shaken as he felt it gave a fresher tasting drink.

Strain: a *cocktail strainer* is a metal sieve that is used to strain the cocktail after mixing to prevent any ice, pulp or fruit juice from ending up in the glass. The strainer is placed in the mouth of the *shaker*, after which the cocktail can be poured into the serving glass. You can also *double strain* to get an extra fine cocktail.

Bar spoon: a *bar spoon* is a thin, long spoon with a twist in the middle that is used for mixing or for adding a layer between alcoholic and non-alcoholic liquids (*layers*). Its length means that you can reach the bottom of even the largest shaker and stir ingredients directly into the glass without having to shake the drink too much. The spoon holds 5 ml of liquid, just as much as a teaspoon. Mixing or stirring ingredients is done in a *mixing glass* with lots of ice. You can create layers in a *shot glass* by pouring ingredients slowly over the rounded edge of the bar spoon and slowly lifting the bar spoon upwards.

About the Belgian Barflies

Ben Wouters met Olivier Jacobs years ago and, thanks to him, began working in the restaurant trade behind the bar of the bar-restaurant *Cafe Theatre* in Ghent. Erik Veldhuis trained within the hospitality industry in the Netherlands and worked as an intern at the *Ghent Marriott Hotel*. He opened a cocktail bar in Ghent, where he came to know Olivier and Ben. Today Ben and Erik are responsible for the bar of restaurant *Volta* in Ghent, while Olivier stood for years behind the bar of *Cafe Theatre*. These days he is his own boss at his own cocktail bar in Ghent: *JIGGER'S, The Noble Drugstore*. During *Bloot!*, a culinary initiative of Flemish foodies Kobe Desramaults (In the Wulf, the Vitrine), Jason Blanckaert (J.E.F.) and Olly Ceulenaere (Volta), the cocktail makers united to become the *Belgian Barflies*. Their philosophy works around their respect for the classic cocktails and they draw inspiration from the cocktails and work of legendary American barmen between 1890 and the period of prohibition. They leaf through books containing old recipes, and give them a modern twist with their own special brand of creativity.

Recipes by Olivier Jacobs

Blood & Smoke

1.5 fl oz / 4.5 cl Tanqueray Ten (a type of gin, made in Scotland)
.66 fl oz / 2 cl Cherry Heering (Danish liqueur with cherry flavor)
.66 fl oz / 2 cl red grapefruit juice
.66 fl oz / 2 cl Carpano Antica Formula (Italian red vermouth)
apple wood smoke

Put all of the ingredients into the glass mixing glass, smoke the inside of the metal part of the shaker with the apple wood (see photo) and shake this with lots of ice. Double strain it into a chilled cocktail glass and garnish with a piece of caramelized red grapefruit.

East-West Punch

1.33 fl oz / 4 cl Don Julio Reposado
.33 fl oz / 1 cl mezcal (100 % agave)
.66 fl oz / 2 cl red grapefruit juice
.85 fl oz / 2.5 cl cranberry syrup
1 fl oz / 3 cl lapsang souchong tea
1.75 fl oz / 5 cl Timmermans gueuze beer

This is really meant to be a punch and is therefore made in a punchbowl. The quantities stated here are for one person. Use large pieces of ice for the punch and add some grapefruit zest and a few slices of lemon.

Mezcal
Mezcal is a Mexican alcoholic drink made from agave fruit. There are various types of agave and each makes a different type of mescal. The most well known is tequila, made from the tequila or blue agave. Don Julio Reposado is also a brand of tequila.

Lapsang souchong tea
The tea leaves used for lapsang souchong are somewhat larger and older than normal. This smoky tea comes from the large leaves of the best China tea and has a strong flavor.

Like a virgin

1.5 fl oz / 4.5 cl Ciroc vodka
1 fl oz / 3 cl verjus
.5 fl oz / 1.5 cl cranberry syrup
2 dashes of eucalyptus bitters (the special pouring spout of the bottle will only pour two drops at a time)
dried orange zest

Place all of the ingredients (apart from the zest) into a mixing glass with ice and stir for twenty seconds. Pour the contents into a chilled cocktail glass and serve under a bell jar full of the smoke of the dried orange zest.

Ciroc vodka
Ciroc is a brand of distilled alcohol from France that is sold as vodka. It's distinguishable from its Russian counterpart by the fact that the drink is made from grapes, as opposed to the more commonly used corn, millet, rye, wheat or potatoes. Because the drink is distilled to 96 percent and does not mature, it has the characteristics of vodka.

31

Eucalyptus bitters

This is a bitter alcoholic drink with a fresh eucalyptus flavor. Before it's bottled, the drink is matured in smoked French oak to create its rich, deep flavor and to nicely finish the aroma. Available at Salon 39 (www.salon39.dk).

Parmanhatten

1.7 fl oz / 5 cl Johnnie Walker Black Label, infused with Parma ham
.66 fl oz / 2 cl Carpano Antica Formula
.33 fl oz / 1 cl Noilly Prat dry
1 bar spoon of Luxardo maraschino
2 dashes orange bitters

Place all of the ingredients into a mixing glass and stir for twenty seconds before straining into a chilled cocktail glass. Garnish with a piece of dried Parma ham.

Luxardo maraschino

Maraschino or marasquin is a bittersweet, clear liqueur made from marasca cherries, a variety of the sour cherry that is grown in the Croatian region of Dalmatia. Maraschino is one of the few liqueurs that are distilled. The distillate is created from both the pulp of the fruit as well as the (broken) pit of the cherry, which gives the liqueur a very specific almond flavor. The distillate matures for two years in Finnish ash wood vats before it's thinned and sweetened. Luxardo is a brand of the liqueur, which has existed since 1821.

Recipes by Ben Wouters

The Ladyboy

.5 fl oz / 1.5 cl vodka, infused with smoked chili
1 good slice of fresh melon (preferably a green honeydew melon)
1.70 fl oz / 5 cl Ketel One vodka
.33 fl oz / 1 cl lime juice
.33 fl oz / 1 cl agave syrup
.33 fl oz / 1 cl batida het coco
2 sprigs of fresh cilantro

Chill the glass in ground or finely crushed ice. Pour the vodka and the smoked chili over the ice and stir the mixture once. Muddle the melon in a mixing glass. Add the other ingredients. Shake everything. Remove the ice from the glass and strain the cocktail into the serving glass. Finish with a slice of melon or a leaf of cilantro.

Cardamango

1/4 ripe mango
fresh black cardamom
1 fl oz / 3 cl Singleton 12 year old
1 fl oz / 3 cl Hayman's Sloe gin
.33 fl oz / 1 cl Becherowka
1 fl oz / 3 cl orange juice
orange zest

Chill the glass in ground or finely crushed ice. Muddle the mango with the cardamom, add the rest of the ingredients and shake hard with the ice cubes. Double strain into a cocktail glass and finish with the orange zest.

Orange Skye
.66 fl oz / 2 cl Talisker, 10 year old
1 fl oz / 3 cl sweet red wine (arynas)
.85 fl oz / 2.5 cl fresh mandarin juice
1 bar spoon of mandarine napoléon
.5 fl oz / 1.5 cl chocolate liqueur

Shake everything together and double strain into a cocktail glass.

Recipes by Erik Veldhuis

The Original Smokey Business
1.35 fl oz / 4 cl Lagavullin, 16 year old
.66 fl oz / 2 cl elderflower, The Bitter Truth
or St-Germain
.33 fl oz / 1 cl fresh apple and pear juice
1 bar spoon of Noilly Prat dry vermouth
orange zest

Stir it all together. Pour it out into a small martini glass and finish with the orange zest.

Spice Up a Smoking Hot Virgin
1.70 fl oz / 5 cl Ketel One Lemon
(infused with sweet chili pepper)
.66 fl oz / 2 cl fresh lemon juice
5 leaves fresh basil
Lea & Perrins Worcestershire Sauce
to serve:
celery salt
black pepper
¾ in / 2 cm cucumber
lemon geranium leaves

Fill a glass to the top with ice and pour in all of the liquids. Pour this mixture into a shaker or mixing glass. Pour it all back into the original glass. This technique is called the roll. Pour the cocktail into a large tumbler. Finish the glass with celery salt and black pepper, two slices of cucumber (or a slice of lemon) and a few leaves of lemon geranium.

Smoked Old Fashioned
.66 fl oz / 2 cl cardamom and cinnamon syrup
1 small dash of soda water, Fever-Tree
2 dashes of old fashioned bitters, Fee Brothers
1.70 fl oz / 5 cl Zapaca, 23 year old, smoked
with cherry wood
orange and lemon zest

Pour everything into a mixing glass and stir with a bar spoon. Serve in an old fashioned glass. Finish with the orange and lemon zest.

33

2
SNACKS

Carpaccio of warm smoked lamb
fillet, grilled garlic tapenade and
dried tomatoes

CARPACCIO OF WARM SMOKED LAMB FILLET, GRILLED GARLIC TAPENADE AND DRIED TOMATOES

 Suitable for:
Closed barbecue, Outdoorchef, Green Egg, Grill Dome, Weber, Boretti, KitchenAid barbecue...

SERVES 4

3/4 cups / 200 g sea salt
1/8 cup / 40 g cane sugar
1/4 cup / 40 g juniper berries, crushed
4 tsps of rosemary, chopped
2 tsps of fresh thyme, chopped
4 cloves
4 tsps of sage, chopped
1.1 lb / 500 g lamb fillet
2 whole heads of garlic
8 tomatoes
Maldon salt (coarse salt flakes)

olive oil
3 sprigs of rosemary, chopped
black pepper

on the closed barbecue:
2 handfuls of smoking chips
1 handful of olive pits

to serve:
6 oz / 150 g sovrano slivers (hard Italian cheese)
1 handful of arugula

Mix the sea salt with the cane sugar, juniper berries rosemary, thyme, cloves and sage. Rub this into the lamb fillet and wrap it in saran wrap. Allow it to marinate in the refrigerator for 12 hours. Slice the heads of garlic in half and grill them until soft. Remove the pulp and mix it into a tapenade. Peel the tomatoes and remove the flesh. Place into an oven-proof dish and sprinkle with some salt, olive oil and the chopped sprigs of rosemary. Leave to dry for 8 hours in the oven at 104 °F / 40 °C. Remove the lamb fillet from the saran wrap, rinse and dry.

Throw the smoking chips and the olive pits onto the barbecue and smoke the lamb fillet for 20 minutes in a closed barbecue at 230 °F / 110 °C. Remove the meat from the heat and allow it to cool down in the freezer. Once it's ice cold, slice it into paper-thin pieces on a plate. Sprinkle it with olive oil, the garlic tapenade, ground black pepper, the sovrano slivers, the dried tomatoes and the arugula.

> LAMB RIBS WITH HOISIN SAUCE AND COUSCOUS

 Suitable for:
Open and closed barbecue, Buck, Bon Fire, Outdoorchef, Boretti, Green Egg, Grill Dome, KitchenAid barbecue...

SERVES 4

1-1/2 cups / 300 g Hoisin Sauce (sweet black bean sauce from China)
4 tsps of Worcestershire sauce
4 tsps of balsamic vinegar
5 cloves of garlic, crushed
1 onion, finely chopped
10 sprigs of fresh thyme
5 sprigs of rosemary
1 chili, finely chopped
4.5 lbs / 2 kg lamb ribs
1 red bell pepper
1 green bell pepper

1 bunch fresh cilantro
1 pack of couscous
pepper and salt
1 can of beer (e.g. Gordon Finest Scotch)
water
5 cloves of garlic
4 bay leaves
5 sprigs of thyme

for the barbecue:
1 handful of wood chips infused with Jack Daniels

Make the marinade by combining the Hoisin Sauce with the Worcestershire sauce and the balsamic vinegar. Add the crushed garlic. Mix the onion with the thyme, rosemary and the chili. Rub this into the ribs and cover them with saran wrap and allow them to marinate in the refrigerator for around 6 hours. Cut the peppers into small pieces and finely chop the cilantro. Prepare the couscous according to the instructions on the package and then mix in the peppers and cilantro before seasoning with salt and pepper.

Place a fireproof dish into the charcoal. Pour in half of the beer and fill the dish up to half its capacity with water. Add the cloves of garlic, the bay leaves and the sprigs of thyme. Place the grill on the barbecue and put the ribs on to that, above the dish of beer. Leave it to cook for 45 minutes under a closed barbecue at 300 °F / 150 °C. Throw the water-soaked wood chips in among the coals or onto the gas grill.

STUFFED PORTOBELLO MUSHROOMS WITH BARBECUE BACON CUBES AND GARDEN VEGETABLES

 Suitable for:
Closed barbecue, Outdoorchef, Le Panyol, Green Egg, Grill Dome, Weber, Boretti, KitchenAid barbecue...

SERVES 4

4 slices of Elckerlijc Farm barbecue bacon,
vegetables, such as celery and bell peppers,
finely chopped
2 shallots
2 cloves of garlic
4 tsps of fresh tarragon leaves, chopped
4 tsps of basil, chopped
8 small portobello mushrooms

herbs for vegetables (see *The basics* on p. 24)
2 fresh mozzarellas
6 oz / 150 g sovrano, grated

for the barbecue:
1 handful of herbs for the fire (see *The basics* on p. 24)

Slice the barbecue bacon, the vegetables and the shallots into small cubes, crush the cloves of garlic into it and mix this with the fresh herbs. Season with the herbs for vegetables and divide the mixture among the eight mushrooms. Place a slice of mozzarella into each portobello and sprinkle over a little sovrano.

Place the mushrooms in a closed barbecue for 10 minutes or into a Le Panyol wood oven until the cheese is melted. Sprinkle the herbs for the fire on the base for aroma.

```
Portobello
This variation of chestnut mushroom was brought
over to Europe from America. A special method of
cultivation means that this type grows to become
a large cap mushroom with a cap of 2 to 5 in / 6 to
12 cm and is ideal for stuffing. The flesh is white,
firm and very aromatic.
```

41

> BIRCH WOOD GRILLED PLAICE ROLLS

 Suitable for:
Closed barbecue, Outdoorchef, Green Egg, Grill Dome, Boretti, Weber, KitchenAid barbecue...

SERVES 4

2 sole in filets (8 pieces)
7 oz / 200 g olive tapenade, or to taste
8 slices of Elckerlijc Farm bacon 8 leaves of basil
8 marinated tomatoes (see recipe for carpaccio of smoked lamb fillet on p. 37)

8 sprigs of rosemary
fish marinade (see *The basics* on p. 25)
herbs for fish (see *The basics* on p. 24)
1 fresh section of birch wood bark

Open up the plaice rolls on the table and spread them with the olive tapenade. Place a slice of bacon, a basil leaf and a tomato on top. Roll them up nice and tight. Remove the needles from the sprigs of rosemary and cut the ends into a point.

Push the skewers through the plaice rolls and rub them with fish marinade. Season with herbs for fish. Place the rolls on the bark over the grill for 20 minutes in a closed barbecue at 480 °F / 250 °C. The flavor of the fresh wood will penetrate the fish.

`TIP` For this recipe you could use olive wood. If the wood is dry, you will first
need to leave it to soak for 12 hours in water before placing it on the fire.

43

PARTY FORMULA
> 2 <

The big party

Who says that a barbecue doesn't go with a communion or an intimate wedding party? Set out a long table in the garden, organize some great live music and treat your guests to an unforgettable dance party. For larger groups, simply opt for larger pieces of meat and fish so that you don't have to cook hundreds of separate portions on the barbecue. Prepare as much as you can ahead of time so that on the day itself all you need to do is take everything out of the fridge. Make sure that you also ask for enough help so that you don't end up doing it all on your own. Put a few colorful bunches of flowers on the tables and make sure there are enough tea lights dotted about the place for when night falls.

QUAIL BREAST WITH CUBERDON CANDIES, SMOKED BACON AND A PUREE OF BUTTERNUT SQUASH

Suitable for:
Open and closed barbecue, Buck, Bon Fire, Outdoorchef, Boretti, Green Egg, Grill Dome, KitchenAid barbecue...

SERVES 4

1/2 butternut squash
olive oil
1 sprig of fresh rosemary, chopped
ground black pepper
Maldon salt (coarse salt flakes)
3/8 in / 1 cm fresh ginger
juice of 1/2 orange
4 cuberdon candies

8 leaves of basil
8 quail breasts
16 slices of smoked bacon, finely sliced
marinade for meat (see *The basics* on p. 25)
herbs for the barbecue (see *The basics* on p. 25)

for on the closed barbecue:
1 handful of wood chips infused with Jack Daniels

Cut the butternut squash into quarters. Sprinkle with olive oil, the chopped rosemary, salt and pepper and place into a closed barbecue for 30 minutes at 350 °F / 180 °C until they are soft. Remove the soft flesh of the squash and mix in a blender with the ginger and the orange juice. Place half of a cuberdon candy and a basil leaf into a quail fillet and then lay another fillet on top of that one. Wrap the smoked bacon around it. Rub with the marinade for meat and season with herbs for the barbecue.

Grill the quail for 10 minutes on the barbecue and throw a handful of water-soaked wood shavings onto the coals. Serve on a puree of butternut.

 TIP You can also rub the quail with cuberdon candy syrup. Place them on a medium barbecue for 10 minutes and you'll have deliciously coated quail fillets!

 TIP If the butternut puree is too wet, thicken it with xanthium gum, a very popular thickening agent available from gourmet food stores.

48

STUFFED POINTED SWEET PEPPERS WiTH FETA CHEESE AND CHORiZO

Suitable for:
Closed barbecue, Outdoorchef, Le Panyol, Green Egg, Grill Dome, Weber, Boretti, KitchenAid barbecue...

SERVES 4

6 black olives, pitted
3.5 oz / 100 g chorizo
6 marinated tomatoes (see recipe for carpaccio of smoked lamb fillet on p. 37)
2 sprigs of basil
7 oz / 200 g feta cheese

herbs for the barbecue (see *The basics* on p. 25)
8 small pointed sweet peppers
8 slices of chorizo
olive oil
herbs for vegetables (see *The basics* on p. 24)

Chop the olives, chorizo, tomatoes and the basil very finely and mix this with the feta and season with herbs for the barbecue. Cut out the white part of the peppers and remove the seeds. Stuff the peppers with the feta mixture and stick a slice of chorizo to it with a wooden toothpick. Rub the peppers with olive oil and season with herbs for vegetables.

Grill the peppers for 6 minutes on a medium grill.

GRILLED ARTICHOKE BOTTOMS WITH BARBECUE BACON AND A MOREL MUSHROOM PUREE

 Suitable for:
Open and closed barbecue, Buck, Bon Fire, Outdoorchef, Boretti, Green Egg, Grill Dome, KitchenAid barbecue...

SERVES 4

1 carrot
1 fennel bulb
1 shallot
8 small artichokes
1-1/4 cups / 3 dl white wine
1-1/4 cups / 3 dl chicken stock
1 star anise
4 sprigs of savory
10 oz / 300 g morel mushroomsolive oil
herbs for vegetables (see *The basics* on p. 24)
4 spring onions

1/4 cup / 40 g butter
1/4 cup / 60 g cream
4 slices of barbecue bacon, Elckerlijc Farm, 1/4 in. /
0.5 cm thick

for the barbecue:
1 handful of herbs for the fire (see *The basics* on p. 24)

to serve:
fresh herbs such as mint or basil
a few edible flowers

Finely chop the carrot, fennel and shallot. Cut off the leaves of the artichokes so that only the bottom remains. Cook the finely chopped vegetables in olive oil and deglaze the pan with the white wine and chicken stock. Add the star anise and the savory and cook the artichokes until al dente in the stock. Allow them to cool in the cooking liquor. Roll the washed morels in the olive oil and grill for 6 minutes on medium hot barbecue. Sprinkle a handful of herbs for the fire under the grill. Chop the spring onions finely and cook them in 2 Tbs of butter. Add the cream and the rest of the butter and combine this mixture with the grilled morels until you have a smooth puree. Smear the artichoke bottoms with olive oil and season them with herbs for vegetables.

Grill the bases for 4 minutes over a medium hot barbecue. Slice the barbecue bacon into strips and divide them over the artichoke bottoms. Add a spoonful of the hot morel puree and decorate with the fresh herbs and flowers.

MINI PIZZAS WITH PUMPKIN PUREE AND ELCKERLIJC FARM BARBECUE BACON

Suitable for:
Le Panyol, closed barbecue, Outdoorchef, Green Egg, Grill Dome, Weber, Boretti, KitchenAid barbecue, etc. with pizza stonE

SERVES 4

3 uncooked pizza crusts, pre-rolled
2/3 cup / 300 g butternut puree (see recipe for quail breast on p. 46)
9 oz / 250 g barbecue bacon, Elckerlijc Farm
7 oz / 200 g chanterelle mushrooms
1 onion, chopped

2 Tbs fresh cilantro, chopped
6 oz / 150 g sovrano, grated

for the barbecue:
1 handful of olive pits

Take 4 in / 10 cm round pizzas. Smear with a spoonful of butternut puree. Slice the bacon into thin strips and sprinkle this over the puree. Wash the chanterelles well in running water and dry them using a kitchen towel. Sprinkle a few mushrooms over the pizzas along with a little onion, cilantro and sovrano.

Cook them in a Le Panyol-wood oven or on a pizza stone in a closed barbecue at 480 °F / 250 °C. Add a handful of olive pits to the fire for a delicious aroma.

GRILLED CHICKEN LIVERS WITH A PUREE OF BELLE DE FONTENAY POTATOES AND ROASTED NUTS

Suitable for:
Closed and open barbecue, Buck, Bon Fire, Outdoorchef, Boretti, Green Egg, Grill Dome, KitchenAid barbecue.

SERVES 4

for the chicken stock:
2.2 lbs / 1 kg chicken necks
2.2 lbs / 1 kg chicken wings
3 star anise
2 tsp / 10 g mace

for the potato puree:
1.1 lbs / 500 g potatoes (belle de fontenay)
1/3 cup / 1 dl chicken stock
2 tsps of sour cream
herbs for vegetables (see *The basics* on p. 24)

for the sauce:
1 leek
2 carrots
2 onions
2 stalks of white celery
2 Tbs of butter

1/4 cup / 50 g brown sugar
1/3 cup / 1 dl dry sherry
1/3 cup / 1 dl sherry vinegar
1 quart / 1 liter chicken stock
1 sprig of thyme
bay leaf
1/3 cup / 75 g butter

for the chicken livers:
16 chicken livers
marinade for meat (see *The basics* on p. 25)
herbs for meat (see *The basics* on p. 25)

for the barbecue:
a handful of herbs for the fire (see *The basics* on p. 24)

to serve:
3.5 oz / 100 g nuts of your choice, toasted

Add everything for the chicken stock to 4 quarts / 4 liters of water and allow to infuse over low heat for 3 hours. Strain the stock. Cook the potatoes gently in the stock, mash them and mix with 1/3 cup / 1 dl of chicken stock and the sour cream. Season with herbs for vegetables. Fry the vegetables for the sauce in 2 Tbs of butter. Add the sugar and allow to caramelize. Deglaze the pan with the sherry and the sherry vinegar. Add the chicken stock, thyme and bay leaf and allow to cook. Assemble with the butter.

Rub the chicken livers with the marinade for meat and season with herbs for meat. Grill them for 5 minutes on a hot barbecue. Sprinkle a handful of herbs for the fire under the grill for a delicious aroma. Place the chicken livers on top of the potato puree and pour over a scant tablespoon of the sauce and dust with chopped nuts.

> SATAY OF BOUDIN NOIR AND BOUDIN BLANC WITH A PUREE OF ROASTED MACADAMIA NUTS

 Suitable for:
Open and closed barbecue, Buck, Bon Fire, Outdoorchef, Boretti, Green Egg, Grill Dome, KitchenAid barbecue

SERVES 4

2 boudins blancs
2 boudins noirs
1 bunch of sage
1.5 oz / 40 g macadamia nuts
3.5 oz / 100 g artichokes, grilled (see recipe for grilled artichoke bottoms on p. 51)
2/3 cup / 125 g cream

2 Tbs of butter
salt and pepper
marinade for meat (see *The basics* on p. 25)

for the barbecue:
1 handful of herbs for the fire (see *The basics* on p. 24)

Slice the sausages into pieces 3/16 in / 1 cm thick and spear them onto a skewer in alternate colors, placing a sage leaf in-between each one. Grill the nuts over a hot barbecue and throw a handful of herbs for the fire onto the coals. Mix the nuts with the artichokes, the cream, the butter and a pinch salt and pepper.

Rub the kebabs with the marinade for meat and grill them briefly over a hot barbecue. Serve with the puree of macadamia nuts.

Thai chicken satay

THAI CHICKEN SATAY

Suitable for:
Open and closed barbecue, Buck, Bon Fire, Weber…

SERVES 4
1.1 lbs / 500 g chicken fillet

for the marinade:
1/3 cup / 1 dl water
1/3 cup / 1 dl soy sauce
juice of 1 lime
4 tsps of grated galangal root (or ginger)
2 cloves of garlic, grated
1 green chili, finely chopped

for the sauce:
7/8 cup / 2 dl coconut milk
1 tsp of paprika
4 spring onions, chopped
2 tsps of cilantro, chopped
2 tsps of peanut butter
1 pinch salt

for the barbecue:
lemongrass stalks (for skewering the chicken)
1 handful of herbs for the fire (see *The basics* on p. 24)

Slice the chicken fillet into strips 3/16 in / 1 cm thick. Combine everything for the marinade and leave the chicken strips in this for 12 hours. Slice the lemongrass stalks with a very sharp knife. Skewer the chicken strips onto these in a loop shape. Place everything for the sauce into a stainless-steel pan and cook for around 4 minutes. Grill the kebabs for 5 minutes over a medium hot grill and throw the herbs for the fire onto the coals or the gas barbecue. Serve with the hot sauce.

59

PARTY FORMULA

> 3 <

On a hot summer day

A sweltering, lazy summer's day demands a relaxed barbecue party by the pool. Invite a few friends over; impromptu parties are always the most fun! A great device for this kind of summer barbecue is the Buck. This open barbecue comes in cheerful colors such as Mr. Black, Mr. Blue, Mr. White and Mr. Orange, and is incredibly appealing. You can of course use any kind of barbecue grill, as long as the atmosphere is good!

SHRIMP WITH PAPAYA CHUTNEY SMOKED AT THE TABLE WITH PATCHOULI

 Suitable for:
Open barbecue, Buck, Bon Fire, Weber...

SERVES 4

1/3 cup / 1 dl rice oil
2 tsps of patchouli leaves, fresh where possible
8 shrimp

for the chutney:
2.2 lbs / 1 kg papaya
2 oz / 60 g fresh ginger

4 red chili peppers, seeded
2/3 cup / 200 g honey
1 cup / 2.5 dl white wine vinegar (muscadet)
2 Tbs of fresh basil, chopped

for the barbecue:
2 tsps of patchouli leaves, dried

Heat the rice oil to boiling and then remove from heat. Add the patchouli leaves to the oil and leave to cool. Peel the shrimp and marinate them in the oil for 24 hours. Peel the papayas and slice into 3/4 in / 2 cm pieces. Slice the ginger and chili peppers into a fine julienne. Add to a pot with the honey and the white wine vinegar. Heat everything and allow to cook over very low heat for 1 hour. At the very last moment, add the basil. Leave to cool.

Put a scant tablespoon of chutney into each glass. Grill the shrimp for 5 minutes over a hot grill. Put two shrimp into each glass, blow in the patchouli smoke using a smoking gun covered with a lid and then serve.

TARTARE OF WEST FLEMISH RED BEEF SMOKED WITH PATCHOULI LEAVES AND TRUFFLE CAVIAR

 Suitable for:
Closed barbecue, KitchenAid barbecue, Weber...

SERVES 4

7 oz / 200 g West Flemish Red beef, fat and
membrane removed
5 chanterelle mushrooms
1 shallot, finely chopped
1 tsp ketchup
1 tsp mayonnaise
1 tsp Worcestershire sauce
1 tsp pesto

ground pepper
1 pinch Maldon salt
3.5 oz / 100 g fresh goose liver (optional)
1.75 oz / 50 g truffle caviar

for the barbecue:
4 tsps of dried patchouli leaves
4 tsps of smoking chips

Slice the meat with a very sharp knife into thin strips and then into small blocks and then into a fine tartare. Place the meat in a small dish.

Put the smoke shavings and the patchouli leaves into a smoke generator and cold-smoke the meat for 30 minutes (max. 98.6 °F / 37 °C) with a smoke generator in a barbecue or in the smoking chamber. Wash the chanterelles and chop fine. Using a fork, combine the meat with the shallot, the mushrooms, the ketchup, the mayonnaise, the Worcestershire sauce and the pesto and season with salt and pepper. Divide the meat into four small pots (you could use the empty caviar pots). Top (if you like) with a thin slice of goose liver and cover with a thin layer of truffle caviar.

 Delicious with a salad.

3

FiSH DISHES

> WHOLE SALMON IN DILL SAUCE

 Suitable for:
Closed barbecue, Outdoorchef, Le Panyol, Green Egg, Grill Dome, Weber, Boretti, KitchenAid barbecue...

SERVES 4

2/3 cup / 150 ml water
1.7 oz / 50 g Point-Virgule instant marinade for fish
2.2 lbs / 1 kg salmon
herbs for fish (see *The basics* on p. 24)
1 bunch of dill
3 limes
4 sprigs of thyme
6 bay leaves
1 head of garlic
2 cups / 5 dl Dominus triple

for the sauce:
1-1/2 cups / 300 g mayonnaise
3/4 cup / 150 g sour cream
juice of 1 lemon
ground pepper
1 pinch sea salt
2 Tbs of dill, chopped

for the barbecue:
1/8 cup / 0.5 dl white wine
1/8 cup / 0.5 dl water

Combine the water and the instant marinade in a bowl and baste the salmon evenly with the marinade. Place the salmon on a grill, rub with the fish marinade and season with herbs for fish. Stuff the stomach cavity with dill, lime, thyme, bay leaf and garlic.

Place a fireproof dish over the charcoal and pour in the white wine and the water. Put the grill on top and then the salmon above the bath of white wine. Allow to cook for around 1 hour. In the meantime, make the sauce from mayonnaise, sour cream, lemon juice, salt and pepper and dill. Serve the salmon with the sauce and salad.

`TIP` The salmon is ready when you can remove the dorsal fin.

FISH DISHES

Fillet of cod with Ganda ham and tomato salad

FILLET OF COD WITH GANDA HAM AND TOMATO SALAD

 Suitable for:
Closed and open barbecue, Buck, Bon Fire, Outdoorchef, Boretti, KitchenAid barbecue, Green Egg, Grill Dome and Le Panyol (amazing result!).

SERVES 4

1.7 oz / 50 g Point-Virgule instant marinade for fish
2/3 cup / 150 ml water
4 cod fillets, 9 oz/ 250 g each
8 thin slices of Ganda ham
4 tomatoes
7 oz / 200 g mozzarella
12 leaves fresh basil
1-3/4 cups / 4 dl olive oil extra virgin (very important for the lovely taste of dish)

7/8 cup / 2 dl balsamic vinegar
fresh ground black pepper (or 4 tsps of ground pepper)
Maldon salt (coarse salt flakes)
herbs for fish (see *The basics* on p. 24)

for the barbecue:
1 handful of herbs for the fire (see *The basics* on p. 24)

Combine the water and instant fish marinade in a bowl and baste the four filets of cod with the marinade. Lay out two slices of the ham for each fillet and wrap these around the pieces of cod. Slice the tomatoes into rounds, place on a plate and cover with the slices of mozzarella and the basil leaves, then pour the extra virgin oil over them. Sprinkle with a few dashes of balsamic vinegar, some ground black pepper and a little Maldon salt. Wrap in saran wrap and allow the flavors to develop for two hours in the refrigerator.

Baste the fish with the fish marinade and some herbs for fish. Place the fish into a fish grill and cook for 8 minutes (for fillets that are around 1-1/2 in / 4 cm thick) above a medium hot barbecue. Consider throwing some herbs for the fire onto the hot coals for a delicious aroma. Serve the fish on the tomato salad, sprinkle with some olive oil and finish with a sprig of greenery.

`TIP` In place of cod, you could also go for wolf fish with Spanish ham.

PLANK GRILLED SALMON FILLET WITH HOMEMADE HERB PESTO

 Suitable for:
Closed barbecue, Outdoorchef, Green Egg, Grill Dome, Weber, KitchenAid barbecue, Boretti...

SERVES 4

for the salmon on a plank:
1 wooden plank made of ash, cedar,
maple or fruit tree
some cloves of garlic for the plank
olive oil
1 salmon fillet weighing 2.3 lbs / 1 kg, with skin on

for the pesto:
3.5 oz / 100 g marinated tomatoes (see recipe for
carpaccio of smoked lamb fillet on p. 37)

7 oz / 200 g fresh garden herbs
2 oz / 50 g walnuts
3.5 oz / 100 g parmesan
2 cloves of garlic
pepper and salt
4 tsps of olive oil

to serve:
7 oz / 200 g lettuce
10 oz / 300 g yellow vine tomatoes

Soak the plank in water for 24 hours, drill a few holes into it and stuff these with cloves of garlic. Rub the plank with olive oil and place the salmon, skin side down, on the plank. Put all of the ingredients for the pesto into a blender and mix. Season with ground pepper and sea salt. Add olive oil until you have a nice pesto.

Rub the salmon fillet with the pesto and place the plank into a closed barbecue for 30 minutes at 345 °F / 175 °C. Serve the salmon with a salad of yellow vine tomatoes.

GRILLED PIKE MARINATED IN GOOSE FAT AND COFFEE WITH CELERIAC AND VANILLA OIL

Suitable for:
Closed and open barbecue, Buck, Bon Fire, Outdoorchef, and KitchenAid barbecue, Boretti, Green Egg, Grill Dome and Le Panyol (amazing result!).

SERVES 4

2.2 lbs / 1 kg goose fat
1 cup of coffee beans
4 pike-perch fillets, each weighing 9 oz / 250 g

for the vanilla oil:
2 vanilla beans
1 quart / 1 liter of olive oil

for the vegetables:
1 celeriac (celery root)
fresh pine needles
4 green bell peppers
4 yellow bell peppers

pepper and salt
1.3 lb / 600 g new potatoes
2 shallots, finely chopped
2 slices of smoked bacon cut into strips
4 sprigs of thyme
1/3 cup / 1 dl white wine
7/8 cup / 2 dl chicken stock
7/8 cup / 2 dl rice oil
herbs for vegetables (see *The basics* on p. 24)

for the barbecue:
1 handful of herbs for the fire (see *The basics* on p. 24)

Melt the goose fat in a pot with the ground coffee beans and bring to a boil. Allow to cool. Place the pike fillets into it once the fat has cooled somewhat and leave to marinate for 24 hours. Cover with saran wrap and place into the refrigerator. Scrape the vanilla from the vanilla beans and add to a jar with the olive oil. Allow to infuse for at least 24 hours. Leaving the skin on, place the celeriac into the charcoal and cover with fresh pine needles. Allow to cook for 2 hours, depending on the size of the celeriac. Prick it with a needle to test how soft it is. In the meantime, grill the peppers until they are blackened. Place the green peppers in a plastic bag and close it. Do the same with the yellow peppers. Take them out after about 20 minutes and remove their skins. Mix them separately in a blender and season with salt and pepper. Cook the new potatoes and place them in a Q-bag with the shallots, the bacon strips, the thyme, the white wine, the chicken stock and the rice oil. Sprinkle with herbs for vegetables and fold twice.

Grill the pike for 6 minutes over a medium hot barbecue at 350 °F / 180 °C and sprinkle a handful of herbs for the fire on the coals. Place the new potatoes next to the fish for 10 minutes. Slice the celeriac into rounds and place the pike on top. Squirt a strip of yellow and green pepper sauce alongside and a dash of vanilla oil on the fish.

75

Hot smoked herring,
sweet and sour
salad with a
beetroot and
citrus reduction

HOT SMOKED HERRING, SWEET AND SOUR SALAD WITH A BEETROOT AND CITRUS REDUCTION

 Suitable for:
Closed barbecue, Outdoorchef, Green Egg, Grill Dome, Weber, KitchenAid barbecue, Boretti.

SERVES 4
4 herring

for the herb mixture:
2.2 lbs / 1 kg sea salt
2/3 cup / 200 g cane sugar
4 tsps of cardamom pods, crushed
the zest of 1 orange, in thin strips
2 tsps of oregano, dried
1-1/2 Tbs / 20 g black peppercorns

for the reduction:
2 beets
zest of 1 grapefruit, 1 lemon and 1 orange

for the salad:
1 cucumber
1 red onion
2 cloves of garlic
2 Tbs of cilantro, chopped
2 tsps of sesame seeds, roasted
2-1/2 Tbs of cane sugar
7/8 cup / 2 dl rice vinegar
1/3 cup / 1 dl rice oil
4 tsps of sesame oil

for the barbecue:
oak and beech bark
olive pits

Rub the herring with the herb mixture and place in the refrigerator for 24 hours. Place the whole beetroot into the charcoal for 30 minutes then chop them and juice in a juicer. Allow the juice to cool with the rest of the citrus fruits. Peel the cucumber and slice into rounds with the red onion. Add the crushed garlic. Mix into the cilantro and the sesame seeds. Melt the cane sugar and add the rice vinegar, rice oil and sesame oil. Combine this with the cucumber salad.

Rinse the herring in cold water and pat dry. Hot smoke them at 203 °F / 95 °C, sprinkling the oak and beech bark chips and the olive pits onto the coals. Serve with the cucumber salad.

PARTY FORMULA

> 4 <

The luxury barbecue

Every now and then it's nice to get out your best dinner service and to really go to town with the decorations. The luxury barbecue is one of those moments that you can use to impress your guests; not only with fine dining, but also by using your loveliest barbecue and showing off your skills. A Green Egg guarantees that 'wow effect' and will charm even the most demanding guests. You can cook almost anything on it and, better still, it looks great. Even most star-rated restaurants have a Green Egg.

Don't forget to throw a few woodchips and other aromatics onto the fire, so that the lovely, green, kettle barbecue creates more atmosphere and gives ingredients a delicious, smoky taste.

THAI STYLE CRAB STUFFED WITH BASMATI RICE

 Suitable for:
Closed barbecue, Outdoorchef, Le Panyol, Green Egg, Grill Dome, Weber, KitchenAid barbecue, Boretti...

SERVES 4

4 crabs
herb stock (see *The basics* on p. 27)
1-1/2 cups / 300 g basmati rice
1 red bell pepper
1 bunch of spring onions
1 stalk of lemongrass
3.5 oz / 100 g Thai pea eggplants (if available from Thai or gourmet food stores)
1 dash of rice oil
4 stalks of Thai basil, finely chopped
2 tsps of harissa
4 tsps of cilantro, chopped

2 tsps of galangal root, chopped
1/3 cup / 1 dl mirin
4 tsps of rice wine vinegar
4 tsps of fish sauce
4 tsps of soy sauce
1/3 cup / 1 dl coconut milk
10 oz / 300 g canned crab meat (best quality), to mix into the rice

for the barbecue:
herbs for the fire (see *The basics* on p. 24)

Cook the crabs for 15 minutes in an herb stock. Meanwhile, cook the rice, drain and rinse under cold water. Remove the underside of the crab shell and then remove all of the meat from inside. Cut off the legs and remove the meat from these also. Finely chop the pepper, spring onions and lemongrass. Cook the vegetables in a wok with a dash of rice oil. Add the rice and stir everything well. Add the rest of the ingredients, including the crabmeat. Stuff the empty crab shells. You can even do this a day in advance.

Place the crab shells into a closed barbecue for 20 minutes at 350 °F/ 180 °C. From time to time, throw a handful of herbs for the fire onto the coals.

PLAICE ROLLS IN LARDO DI COLONNATA WITH A PUREE OF KOHLRABI COOKED IN CHARCOAL

 Suitable for:
Closed and open barbecue, Buck, Bon Fire, and KitchenAid barbecue, Outdoorchef, Boretti, Green Egg, Grill Dome and Le Panyol (amazing result!)

SERVES 4

2 kohlrabi
8 marinated tomatoes (see recipe for carpaccio of smoked lamb fillet on p. 37)
8 leaves of basil
4 plaice filets
8 slices of Lardo di Colonnata (check at gourmet stores or an Italian deli)
2 carrots
2 shallots
4 tomatoes
olive oil

7/8 cup / 2 dl white wine
7/8 cup / 2 dl fish fumet (see *The basics* on p. 27)
ground pepper
sea salt
1/2 tsp of curry powder
a dash of cream
fish marinade (see *The basics* on p. 25)
herbs for fish (see *The basics* on p. 24)

for the barbecue:
herbs for the fire (see *The basics* on p. 24)

Place the kohlrabi onto smoldering coals for 2 hours. In the meantime, wrap the plaice fillet around the marinated tomatoes and basil. Then wrap a slice of the lardo around the fish and secure in place with a toothpick. Chop the carrots and shallots into small cubes. Remove the skin and most of the seeds from the tomatoes. Chop them into small cubes. Simmer the vegetables in a dash of olive oil. Deglaze the pan with the white wine and allow to cool. Add the fish fumet and season with pepper, salt and curry powder. Peel the kohlrabi and mix with a dash of cream in a blender. Rub the plaice rolls with fish marinade and season with herbs for fish.

Grill for around 6 minutes on a medium hot grill at 350 °F / 180 °C; sprinkle a handful of herbs for the fire onto the coals. Serve with the kohlrabi puree and the vegetable sauce.

```
Lardo di Colonnata
Colonnata is a small village located in the Tuscan hills, close to the city of
Carrara, known for its marble. After adding salt, the Colonnata lard matures for
some months in marble basins. Today this lard is protected by an IGP quality
brand. The lardo di Colonnata is made from the back fat of a pig and has a
strong, aromatic flavor that makes it an ideal flavoring.
```

MACKEREL WITH GRILLED EGGPLANT AND LENTILS

Suitable for:
Closed and open barbecue, Buck, Bon Fire, Outdoorchef, and KitchenAid barbecue, Boretti, Green Egg, Grill Dome and Le Panyol (amazing result!)

SERVES 4

2 limes
1 galangal root (or ginger)
4 mackerel
1 large bunch of dill
3 eggplant
6 cloves of garlic
4 sprigs of rosemary
olive oil
4 tsps of red wine vinegar
7 oz / 200 g lentils
2 quarts / 2 liters of chicken stock
1 sprig of thyme
1 bay leaf

4 celery stalks
3 carrots
1 white onion
1 red chili
16 vine tomatoes (or small tomatoes from the garden)
4 tsps of flatleaf parsley, chopped
herbs for vegetables (see *The basics* on p. 24)

for the barbecue:
a handful of olive pits
wood chips from Belgian beer barrels

Slice the limes and the galangal root into rounds. Stuff the stomach cavity of the mackerel with dill, lime and galangal root. Slice the eggplant and the cloves of garlic along the centre and stuff the pieces of garlic into the eggplants. Stick a few sprigs of rosemary into them too. Drizzle liberally with olive oil. Grill for 30 minutes in a closed barbecue and throw a handful of olive pits into the charcoal. Once they are done, remove the pulp of the eggplants and mix in a blender. Keep warm. Cook the lentils in the chicken stock with thyme and the bay leaf. In the meantime, chop the celery, the carrots and the white onion into small cubes. Remove the seeds from the chili and chop finely. Cook the vegetables in a wok with the good splash of olive oil and add the cooked lentils. Season with parsley, herbs for vegetables and the chopped chili.

Grill the mackerel in a fish grill and throw a handful of wood chips from Belgian beer barrels onto the coals or onto the gas barbecue to get a smoky aroma. Fillet the fish and serve with the lentils and a spoonful of eggplant puree.

TUNA IN OLIVE OIL AND A SUMMER SALAD WITH GRILLED BELL PEPPERS

 Suitable for:
Closed and open barbecue, Buck, Bon Fire, Outdoorchef, and KitchenAid barbecue, Boretti, Green Egg, Grill Dome and Le Panyol (amazing result!).

SERVES 4

1.75 lbs / 800 g fresh tuna
herbs for fish (see *The basics* on p. 24)
1 sprig of rosemary
1 sprig of oregano
1 sprig of thyme
1 sprig of bay leaf
1 sprig of sage
6 cloves of garlic, sliced
1 lemon, sliced
1 handful of fresh pine needles (young shoots)
3 quarts / 3 liters olive oil

for the quinoa:
1-1/4 cup / 200 g quinoa
2 ripe avocados

for the salad:
3.5 oz / 100 g long radishes (from the garden)
1.75 oz / 50 g purple cress (or small purple basil leaves)
10.5 oz / 300 g fresh leaf lettuce (from the garden)

for the vinaigrette:
juice of 1 lemon
2 tsps of cumin seeds
olive oil
mature balsamic vinegar

for the barbecue:
olive pits
smoking chips

Season the tuna with herbs for fish and grill briefly over a hot grill. Throw a handful of olive pits over the coals. Place the tuna pieces in a fireproof dish and add the fresh herbs, cloves of garlic, the slices of lemon and the pine needles. Cover in olive oil. Place the dish into a closed barbecue for 30 minutes at 200 °F / 90 °C and regularly add olive pits and a handful of smoking chips to the coals.

Cook the quinoa for 25 minutes in a full pot of water. Rinse under cool running water and allow to drain. Peel the avocados and chop into pieces. Mix into the quinoa. Slice the radishes lengthwise and mix with the lettuce. Finish the salad with the purple cress. Make vinaigrette from lemon juice, cumin seeds, olive oil and balsamic vinegar. Remove the tuna from the oil, break it into large pieces and place on top of the salad with the vinaigrette. Serve with the quinoa.

GRILLED SEA BASS WITH VANILLA POTATOES SMOKED WITH CHICORY ROOT

Suitable for:
Closed and open barbecue

SERVES 4

2.2 lbs / 1 kg potatoes (Belle de Fontenay)
7/8 cup / 2 dl olive oil
pepper and salt
mace
1 vanilla pod
4 leeks (preferably from your own garden)
1.75 lbs / 800 g sea bass, skin on and descaled
fish marinade (see *The basics* on p. 25)

herbs for fish (see *The basics* on p. 24)
herbs for vegetables (see *The basics* on p. 24)
2 tsps fine chicory

for the barbecue:
1 handful of olive pits
glass dome for smoking

Boil or steam the potatoes. Mash them to a puree and season with olive oil, pepper, salt and mace. Slice the vanilla pod open, remove the seeds and mix into the potato puree. Slice the leeks into 1-1/2 in / 4 cm sections and steam them until al dente.

Rub the four sea bass with fish marinade and season with herbs for fish. Grill the sea bass for around 8 minutes in a fish grill. Rub the leeks with fish marinade and season with herbs for vegetables. Grill them for 4 minutes alongside the fish. Throw a handful of olive pits onto the coals for the aroma. Serve the fish on a bed of potato puree and lay the leeks alongside. Cover with a glass dome and blow chicory smoke into it using a smoke gun. Sprinkle a little more olive oil on top.

TIP If you do not have a smoke gun, you can light a piece of dry licorice root and place it under the dome or you could first cold smoke the fish for an hour using the cold smoke generator with chicory root.

smoked salmon with
horseradish sauce

> SMOKED SALMON WITH HORSERADISH SAUCE

The best thing to use here is a cold smoke generator. When smoking things, there is often the temptation to create a big fire to light the woods chips. Thanks to this piece of equipment it's possible to moderate the temperature. You fill it with chips made from oak or beech and you can also mix some herbs for the fire or olive pits in with it too. You light a tea light underneath it so that the smoking chips slowly begin to smoke. Place the generator underneath the barbecue, rather than charcoal, or underneath the gas barbecue. Lay the salmon on the grill and close the barbecue. The salmon can now smoke for around 3 hours.

Suitable for:
Closed barbecue.

 TIP You can also use a smoke generator to smoke types of hard cheese and then grate them over pasta. You can also use this technique to smoke fresh goose liver and give it a fantastic flavor without drying out the meat too much.

SERVES 4
1 salmon fillet

for the salt mixture:
2.2 lbs 1 kg coarse sea salt
1 cup / 200 g cane sugar
1/3 cup / 100 g coriander seeds
2 tsp / 10 g mustard seeds
1-1/2 Tbs / 20 g black peppercorns
2 Tbs / 30 g basil, dried
zest of 1 lime (of lemon)

for the sauce:
7/8 cup / 2 dl sour cream
1 shallot
2 tsps of grated horseradish
2 tsps of chopped parsley
pepper and salt

to serve:
slices of ciabatta, toasted

Combine all of the ingredients for the salt mixture and rub the salmon fillet with a thick layer of this mixture. Wrap the fish in saran wrap and marinate it for 24 hours under pressure in the refrigerator. Rinse it under running water and allow it to dry for a few hours.

Cold smoke the salmon at 95 °F / 35 °C for around 3 hours, depending on the desired level of smokiness. Combine all of the ingredients for the sauce. Serve the salmon in thick slices with the toasted ciabatta and a little sauce.

4

MEAT DISHES

ENTRECOTE WITH A JAPANESE VEGETABLE DISH

 Suitable for:
Open barbecue, Buck, Bon Fire (or leave the top off of your closed barbecue)

SERVES 4

1 Chinese cabbage
2 leeks
7 oz / 200 g shitake mushrooms
7 oz / 200 g spinach
6 young carrots
6 spring onions
2.66 lbs / 1.2 kg entrecote (rib eye)
marinade for meat (see *The basics* on p. 25)
herbs for meat (see *The basics* on p. 25)
rice oil

for the sauce:

2-1/2 Tbs of brown sugar
2/3 cup / 1.5 dl sake
2/3 cup / 1.5 dl soy sauce
1 cup / 2.5 dl water
2 tsps of Szechuan pepper, crushed
4 tsps fresh cilantro, chopped

for the barbecue:

1 handful of herbs for the fire (see *The basics* on p. 24)
1 handful of beer keg chips, soaked in water

Clean the vegetables and slice them into rounds. Rub the meat with the marinade for meat and season with herbs for meat. Take a wok topper (wok with holes), pour a little rice oil over the vegetables and cook them briefly in the wok topper over a hot grill. Place a wok onto the heat and allow the brown sugar to melt with a dash of sake and soy sauce. Deglaze, once the mixture has caramelized, with the rest of the soy sauce and the sake and the water. Allow it to reduce a little and then add the pepper and the fresh cilantro.

Throw a handful of herbs for the fire into the coals. Grill the entrecote for 8 minutes over a medium hot grill at 350 °F / 180 °C. Throw a few beer keg chips on to the coals or the gas barbecue. Serve the vegetables in the sauce with the meat cut into strips

 TIP This dish is tasty with a little fried rice.

> **Szechuan pepper**
> This spice is named for the Chinese province of Szechuan, known for its spicy cuisine. Szechuan pepper is in fact not pepper at all, but related to the citrus fruit family. It's notable for its delicate, lemony flavor.

SALTIMBOCCA OF GRILLED VEAL STEAKS WITH ELCKERLIJC FARM BARBECUE HAM

 Suitable for:
Open and closed barbecue, Buck, Bon Fire, Outdoorchef, KitchenAid barbecue, Boretti, Green Egg, Grill Dome

SERVES 4

8 veal steaks, 3 oz / 80 g each, flattened by the butcher
1 bunch of fresh sage from the garden
4 slices of Elckerlijc Farm barbecue ham 3 eggplants
6 cloves of garlic
olive oil
herbs for vegetables (see *The basics* on p. 24)
1.33 lbs / 600 g fresh linguine
4 beefsteak tomatoes

1 onion
ground pepper
sea salt
marinade for meat (see *The basics* on p. 25)
herbs for the barbecue (see *The basics* on p. 25)
4 tsps of fresh basil, chopped

for the barbecue:
olive pits

Take two pieces of meat and place a slice of ham on top of one of them. Cover with the sage leaves and then place the other piece of veal on top of this. Set aside. Slice the eggplants lengthwise and push 2 cloves of garlic into each half. Rub with olive oil and grill in a closed barbecue (or, better still, in a Green Egg) until soft. In the meantime, throw a handful of olive pits onto the coals or the gas grill for a delicious aroma. Remove the pulp from the eggplants with a spoon and puree in a blender with the herbs for vegetables (or salt and pepper). Cook the pasta until al dente and rinse under cool running water. Remove the skins from the tomatoes and chop them into large pieces. Chop the onion and cook it in a wok with some olive oil. Add the pieces of tomato and the eggplant puree to the onions, heat and stir. Season with ground pepper and pinch of sea salt. Add the cooked pasta.

Rub the veal steaks with marinade for meat and sprinkle the herbs for the barbecue on top. Grill them for 6 minutes over a medium hot barbecue. Throw another handful of olive pits onto the coals for a delicious aroma. Serve the meat with the pasta and finish with fresh chopped basil.

saltimbocca of grilled veal
steaks with Elckerlijc Farm
barbecue ham

ROAST PORK WITH HERBY RATATOUILLE IN A Q-BAG

 Suitable for:
Closed barbecue, Outdoorchef, Green Egg, Grill Dome, Weber, KitchenAid barbecue, Boretti...

SERVES 4

2/3 cup / 150 ml water
1.75 oz / 50 g instant marinade for meat
pork joint weighing 2.2 lbs / 1 kg
marinade for meat (see *The basics* on p. 25)
herbs for the barbecue (see *The basics* on p. 25)
4 large potatoes, cooked with the skins on
3.5 oz / 100 g soft herb cheese, of your choice
1 eggplant
1 red bell pepper
1 green bell pepper
1 yellow bell pepper
4 shallots

1 yellow zucchini
4 cloves of garlic
1 fennel
4 tomatoes
2 tsps of cumin seeds
herbs for vegetables (see *The basics* on p. 24)
1-3/4 cups / 4 dl white wine
1-3/4 cups / 4 dl Mexican ketchup

for the barbecue:
grape vine chips, soaked in water
2 Q-bags

Combine the water and the instant marinade in a bowl and baste the marinade evenly across the meat. Rub the meat with marinade for meat, season with herbs for the barbecue and place it on the barbecue for 40 minutes over a medium hot temperature (350 °F / 180 °C). Throw a handful of grape vine chips onto the coals.

Remove the inside of the potatoes with a spoon and mix this with the soft herb cheese. Refill the potatoes and then place them next to the meat for 30 minutes. Clean the vegetables and chop them into large pieces. Slice the cloves of garlic into rounds and the tomatoes into quarters. Season with cumin seeds and herbs for vegetables. Divide all of this between the Q-bags and then add half of the white wine and Mexican ketchup to each of the Q-bags. Close the Q-bags and place them on the barbecue for 20 minutes.

```
Q-bag
When preparing a dish en papillote, you can't easily see if it's ready. That
is why I developed the Q-bag a few years ago. You can completely seal the
package and because of the window on top it's easy to keep track. When you
serve the dish, open this window at the table so that all the scents and
flavors of the ingredients are dispersed and your guests are guaranteed to be
looking forward to dinner.
```

PARTY FORMULA

> 5 <

Formal family party

Got the in-laws or an aunt and uncle coming to visit? Time to get out a classic outdoor gas kitchen like the Outdoorchef. On the one hand it's a closed gas kettle barbecue that can be used for grilling meat, fish or vegetables and, on the other hand, it has a cook-plate for preparing side dishes or sauces. Not only will your visitors be impressed by the device, but you'll make delicious meals. A linen tablecloth gives the table a chic feel.

Q-bag

LEG OF LAMB IN A SALT CRUST

 Suitable for:
Closed barbecue, Outdoorchef, Green Egg, Grill Dome, Weber, KitchenAid barbecue, Boretti...

SERVES 4

1.75 oz / 50 g instant marinade powder for meat
3/4 cup / 175 ml water
leg of lamb weighing 2.2 lbs / 1 kg
herbs for meat (see *The basics* on p. 25)
5-1/8 cups / 1.5 kg coarse sea salt
1-3/4 cups / 0.5 kg kitchen salt
2/3 cup / 80 g flour
6 egg whites
4 sprigs of fresh sage
4 sprigs of rosemary
4 sprigs of thyme
16 new potatoes, pre-cooked
16 slices of smoked bacon
16 bay leaves (optional)
herbs for vegetables (see *The basics* on p. 25)

1 green bell pepper
1 yellow bell pepper
1 red bell pepper
1 red onion
1 zucchini
olive oil
Herbes de Provence
1-3/4 cups / 4 dl white wine
6 fresh ripe tomatoes, chopped
4 tsps of tomato puree

for the barbecue:
herbs for the fire (see *The basics* on p. 24)
Jack Daniels infused wood shavings

Combine the marinade powder with the water and baste the leg of lamb completely with the marinade. Rub the lamb with the same marinade for meat and season with herbs for meat. Combine the salt with the flour, egg whites and the finely chopped sage, rosemary and thyme. Cover the entire joint with a thick layer of salt and place in an oven dish. Place the dish into a closed barbecue for 1 hour and throw lots of herbs for the fire and wood shavings onto the fire to give a lovely flavor to the salt crust.

Roll the potatoes in the bacon and skewer them. You could also add a bay leaf for decoration. Rub with the marinade for meat and season with herbs for vegetables. Leave to marinate for 20 minutes. In the meantime, slice the peppers, onion and zucchini. Cook them in a generous dash of olive oil and season with herbs for vegetables and Herbes de Provence. Deglaze the pan with the white wine, add the tomatoes and the tomato puree and allow to cook. Grill the potato kebabs for 5 minutes alongside the leg of lamb. Remove the lamb from the salt crust and slice into medallions. Serve with the potato kebabs and the sauce.

TURKEY FILLET WITH GRILLED MANGO

Suitable for:
Both a closed or open barbecue, Buck, Bon Fire, Outdoorchef, KitchenAid barbecue, Boretti, Green Egg, Grill Dome.

SERVES 4

2/3 cup / 150 ml water
1.75 oz / 50 g instant marinade for poultry
2.2 lbs / 1 kg turkey fillet
marinade for meat (see *The basics* on p. 25)
herbs for the barbecue (see *The basics* on p. 25)
1/3 cup / 100 g honey
1/4 cup / 50 g hazelnut oil

2 star anise
1 vanilla pod
1-1/2 Tbs / 30 g golden syrup
4 mangos

for the barbecue:
1 handful of herbs for the fire (see *The basics* on p. 24)

Combine the water and the instant marinade in a bowl. Slice the turkey fillet into four good sized pieces. Baste these with the marinade. Rub the filets once more with marinade for meat and season with herbs for the barbecue. Heat the honey in a pan and add the hazelnut oil, star anise and the opened vanilla pod and cook for 1 minute. Then add the syrup and remove from the heat. Peel the mangos and slice them to the pit along their length so that you have eight good sized halves. Place the halved mangos in the honey sauce (you could also do this the day before).

Grill the turkey fillets for 1 to 2 minutes over a medium hot barbecue. Place the mango on the grill for around 10 minutes. You will get an extra tasty roasted flavor if you thrown some herbs for the fire on to the coals.

`TIP` You can best baste all kinds of poultry with instant marinade for poultry.
And the meat will never dry out during grilling.

105

GRILLED RUMP OF VENISON WITH ITALIAN BACON AND SAVOY CABBAGE

 Suitable for:
Closed barbecue, Outdoorchef, Green Egg, Grill Dome, Weber, KitchenAid barbecue, Boretti.

SERVES 4

2/3 cup / 150 ml water
1.7 oz / 50 g instant marinade for game
1 rump of venison, weighing 2.2 lbs / 1 kg
marinade for meat (see *The basics* on p. 25)
herbs for meat (see *The basics* on p. 25)
2 shallots
1-1/4 cups / 3 dl red wine
2 sprigs of thyme
2 bay leaves
7/8 cup / 2 dl game stock
pepper and salt

1 knifepoint of cardamom
20 slices of Italian bacon (pancetta)
1/2 savoy cabbage
2 tablespoons butter
mace (or massis banda, related to nutmeg, available where gourmet herbs are sold, or herbs for vegetables)

for the barbecue:
1 handful of beer keg chips, soaked in water

Combine the water and the instant marinade in a bowl and baste the marinade evenly over the meat. Rub the meat with marinade for meat and season with herbs for meat. Grill the meat for 45 minutes in a medium hot barbecue at 350 °F / 180 °C. Throw a handful of beer keg chips onto the coals.

Chop the shallots, add them to the wine, thyme and bay leaf in a stainless-steel pan and reduce by a third. Add the game stock and season with pepper, salt and cardamom. Slice the bacon into strips. Slice the leaves of the cabbage into the desired shape. Cook the bacon and the cabbage in a generous 2 Tbs of butter and season with pepper, salt and mace (or massis banda, or herbs for vegetables).

```
Massis banda and mace
The Banda Islands form a small group of volcanic islands in the
Banda Ocean and belong to the Indonesian Molucca Islands. Until the
mid-eighteenth century, the Banda Islands were the only source of
spices such as nutmeg and mace, the dried seedpod of the nutmeg.
Nutmeg — actually not a nut at all, but the seed of a firm fruit —
is now available from Malaysia, Sumatra and the Antilles. Massis
banda is the most refined and aromatic variety of nutmeg.
```

Grilled rump of venison with
Italian bacon and savoy cabbage

GRILLED PHEASANT WITH CHICORY AND SMOKED BACON

Suitable for:
Closed and open barbecue, Buck, Bon Fire, Outdoorchef, KitchenAid barbecue, Boretti, Green Egg, Grill Dome

SERVES 4

1.75 oz / 50 g instant marinade for game
2/3 cup 150 ml water
2 pheasants
12 heads of chicory
marinade for meat (see *The basics* on p. 25)
herbs for meat (see *The basics* on p. 35)
butter
juice of 1 lemon
7/8 cup / 2 dl Champagne
1-3/4 cups / 4 dl game stock (or chicken stock)

pepper and salt
8 slices of smoked bacon + 4 slices for drying
herb oil of choice
mace (or herbs for vegetables)

for the barbecue:
1 beer
a little water
1 handful of olive pits
herbs for the fire (see *The basics* on p. 24)

Combine the water and the instant marinade in a bowl and baste the two pheasants until everything is divided evenly. Stuff each pheasant with two heads of chicory. Rub the pheasant with the marinade for meat and season with herbs for meat. Place the pheasant into a closed barbecue for 1 hour at 350 °F / 180 °C over a fireproof dish containing the beer and a little water. Throw a handful of olive pits onto the coals for an extra lovely aroma.

Place the rest of the chicory in a buttered casserole dish, add the juice of the lemon and a little water and cover with parchment paper. Place a small lid on this and then a weight on top of the lid and then allow to cook over low heat. Remove the chicory after about 30 minutes and add the Champagne and the stock. Allow it to cook through. Season with salt and pepper and thicken if necessary with a roux. Wrap the chicory in the bacon and rub them with herb oil. Season with some mace or herbs for vegetables. Grill the vegetables for 6 minutes, turning regularly. Throw some herbs for the fire onto the coals or the grill for a delicious roasted aroma. Keep the vegetables warm under aluminum foil. Now grill the pheasant for 10 minutes on a medium hot barbecue at 350 °F / 180 °C. Put the vegetables onto the plate and place the pheasant on top, cut into slices.

PORK TENDERLOIN GRILLED IN PINE TREE BARK WITH GRASS AND GARDEN HERB PESTO

Suitable for:
Closed barbecue, Outdoorchef, Le Panyol, Green Egg, Grill Dome, Weber, KitchenAid barbecue, Boretti...

SERVES 4

for the pesto:
1 oz / 30 g portobello mushrooms
2 Tbs of fresh ginger, finely chopped
1 shallot, chopped
1-1/2 Tbs / 20 g hazelnuts, roasted
1-1/2 Tbs / 20 g pumpkin seeds, roasted
1-1/2 cups / 50 g flatleaf parsley
1-1/2 cups / 50 g cilantro
1-1/2 cups / 50 g basil
juice of 1 lemon
1 cup / 2.5 dl olive oil
pepper and sea salt

for the meat:
2 large pork tenderloins (preferably organic)
2 pieces of pine tree bark
a handful of long grass from the garden

for the salad:
wild garden herbs, your choice
edible flowers

Place all of the ingredients for the pesto into a blender and mix until you have a rough paste. Cut the tenderloin open along its length, but not so much as to cut it in half fully, just enough to make a flat lap of meat. Rub the pesto over the meat and then roll it into a nice roulade. Cook the tree bark for 3 hours in water and then place it immediately in cold water. Place a piece of the tree bark on the table with a handful of grass and then place the pork tenderloin on top of this. Then put another layer of grass on top and cover it all with the other piece of bark.

Bind this with string and place it into a closed barbecue for 1 hour at 320 °F / 160 °C. Remove the pork tenderloin and serve it with a fresh summer salad of wild garden herbs and flowers.

SADDLE OF LAMB GRILLED OVER TIMMERMANS GUEUZE BEER WITH GARDEN VEGETABLES IN A Q-BAG

Suitable for:
Closed and open barbecue, Buck, Bon Fire, Outdoorchef, and KitchenAid barbecue, Boretti, Green Egg, Grill Dome and Le Panyol (amazing result!)

SERVES 4

6 sprigs of thyme, finely chopped
6 sprigs of tarragon, finely chopped
3 sprigs of sage, finely chopped
5 cloves of garlic, finely chopped
2 Tbs of breadcrumbs
1 whole saddle of lamb
herbs for meat (see *The basics* on p. 25)
a bottle of gueuze beer, Timmermans
fresh seasonal vegetables from your own garden
such as carrots, cabbage, peppers, tomatoes, eggplant
herbs for vegetables (see *The basics* on p. 24)
4 tsps of flatleaf parsley, finely chopped
7/8 cup / 2 dl chicken stock

for the sauce:
2 shallots, finely chopped
2 Tbs of butter
2 tsps of mustard
7/8 cup / 2 dl gueuze beer, Timmermans
1-1/4 cups / 3 dl lamb stock
pepper and salt

for the barbecue:
1 handful of beer keg chips, soaked in water for 15 minutes
1 Q-bag

Remove the thyme, tarragon and sage leaves from the stems and mix with the garlic and the breadcrumbs. Season the saddle of lamb with herbs for meat and cover with the herb crust. Combine the beer with some water in a fireproof dish and place onto the charcoal. Place the grill on top of this, and the saddle of lamb on to the grill. Throw the beer keg chips onto the coals and leave the meat to grill for 30 minutes.

Slice the vegetables and season with herbs for vegetables. Place them into a Q-bag with the flatleaf parsley and the chicken stock. Close it and place it onto the grill for 10 minutes until the vegetables are cooked. Fry the shallots in a stainless-steel pan with the butter. Add the mustard, deglaze the pan with the beer and reduce by half. Pour into the stock and allow to thicken. Season with salt and pepper. Serve the meat with the vegetables and the sauce.

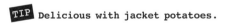 `TIP` Delicious with jacket potatoes.

PARTY FORMULA

> 6 <

Good combos

Invite some old friends or old classmates over and use a cozy Grill Dome. The appealing red ceramic barbecue has its own sense of warmth and conviviality. It works on the same principle as a Green Egg, but is a little less well known than its popular little green brother. Put a couple of cold beers on the table and keep the table linen young and bright. It's a nice idea to serve your dishes on slabs of slate: it's original and looks great.

SPICY THAI CHICKEN

 Suitable for:
Closed and open barbecue, Buck, Bon Fire, Outdoorchef, KitchenAid barbecue, Boretti, Green Egg, Grill Dome.

SERVES 4

6 chicken bottoms

for the green curry:
1/2 tsp of coriander seeds
1/2 tsp of cumin seeds
4 lime leaves
7/8 cup / 2 dl coconut milk
4 shallots
3 spring onions, chopped
2 green chili peppers
1 stalk of lemongrass

2 cloves of garlic, chopped
1-1/2 Tbs of fresh cilantro, chopped
2 tsps of sea salt
3/4 in / 4 cm galangal root (or ginger)

for the sauce:
1 onion, finely chopped
rice oil
2 tsps of green curry paste
7/8 cup / 2 dl chicken stock
7/8 cup / 2 dl coconut milk

Place the coriander and the cumin seeds into a stainless-steel pan and heat them to release their aroma. Then crush them to a powder with the lime leaves and the rest of the ingredients for the green curry. Remove the seed from the chili peppers.

Rub the chicken bottoms with the green curry paste and grill them for 20 minutes over a medium hot barbecue. Place a pot onto the heat, into which you place the chopped onion and generous dash of rice oil. Add the green curry and deglaze the pan with the chicken stock. Allow to cook through and add the coconut milk. Allow to thicken. At the last moment, add the chicken bottoms to finish cooking in the sauce.

TIP Delicious with fried rice.

JAMAICAN CHICKEN WITH RICE

 Suitable for:
Closed barbecue, Outdoorchef, KitchenAid barbecue, Boretti, Green Egg, Grill Dome, Weber.

SERVES 4

2/3 cup / 150 ml water
1.75 oz / 50 g instant marinade for poultry
1 chicken weighing 2.2 lbs / 1 kg
2 apples
Caribbean marinade (or marinade for meat)
2-3/4 cups / 500 g rice
thyme
bay leaf
pepper and salt

3 bunchs of onions
1 chili
2 Tbs of butter
2 cloves of garlic
14 oz / 400 g canned white beans
7/8 cup / 2 dl olive oil
1/3 cup / 1 dl white wine vinegar
herbs for vegetables (see *The basics* on p. 24)
1 cinnamon stick

Combine the water and the instant marinade in a bowl and baste the marinade evenly over the breast of the chicken. Slice the (unpeeled) apples and place them inside the chicken. Rub the chicken with the Caribbean marinade. Place the chicken onto the barbecue for 1 hour at 392 °F / 200 °C. Make sure there is not too much charcoal directly under the chicken (or place a dish with beer under the chicken) to ensure it does not burn. If using a gas barbecue, you should turn off the centre burner.

Cook the rice in water with thyme and bay leaf. Season with salt and pepper. Rinse the rice in cold running water. Finely chop the bunch of onions, remove the seeds from the chili and chop that finely as well. Fry the onions and the chili for 2 minutes in the butter. Crush the garlic into this and combine everything with the rice. Drain the beans and combine them with the rice and olive oil and the white wine vinegar. Season with herbs for vegetables and cook the cinnamon stick with the rice in a wok. Serve the chicken with the rice dish.

MUSTARD FLAVORED ELCKERLIJC FARM BACON WITH TARRAGON STEWED IN A LA TERRA POT WITH DARK 'BOURGOGNE DES FLANDRES' BEER

Suitable for:
Closed barbecue, Le Panyol...

SERVES 4

4.5 lbs / 2 kg pork belly with rind
2/3 cup / 200 g mustard
barbecue seasoning (see *The basics* on p. 25)
bunch of tarragon
meat marinade (see *The basics* on p. 25)
Herbes de Provence
1.1 lb / 500 g potatoes (Belle de Fontenay)
3 carrots
2 leeks
4 turnips
1 swede
2 red onions

good chunk of butter
2 bottles of brown ale, Bourgogne
des Flandres for example
7/8 cup / 2 dl of brown broth
thyme
laurel
rosemary

for the barbecue:
A handful of beer barrel chips,
soaked in water

Ask the butcher to debone the pork belly and put it on the table, rind facing down. Rub in the mustard and barbecue seasoning and scatter the tarragon over the meat. Roll up and tie with string. Rub in the meat marinade and add some more barbecue seasoning. To finish, sprinkle the meat with Herbes de Provence. Grill the meat over high heat on all sides, adding some beer barrel chips to the barbecue.

Clean the potatoes and vegetables. Cut them in large chunks and place them, with the butter, in a De La Terra casserole. Put the grilled meat on top and add the beer, stock, thyme, laurel and rosemary and leave to simmer in a closed barbecue for one hour.

La Terra-pot

TAGINE OF GRILLED LAMB, TURNIPS AND BABY SPINACH

 Suitable for:
Open and closed barbecue, Le Panyol...

SERVES 4

shoulder of lamb, approx. 3.33 lbs / 1.5 kg
meat marinade (see *The basics* on p. 25)
meat spices (see *The basics* on p. 25)
2 onions
4 young carrots
3/4 in / 2 cm fresh ginger
olive oil
2 cups / 0.5 liters vegetable stock

14 oz / 400 g turnips, from your own garden
1.1 lbs / 500 g baby spinach, from your own garden
pepper and salt
1 tsp Ras el hanout
2 tbsp flat parsley, chopped

for the barbecue:
A handful of vine wood chips, soaked in water

Ask the butcher to debone the shoulder of lamb. Chop the meat into 3/4 in / 4 cm chunks, rub on the marinade and season with the meat spices. Grill over a high heat and scatter some vine wood chips on the grill. After 10 minutes, take the meat off the grill. Now cut the onions and carrots into big chunks. Finely chop the ginger and mix with the onions. Add a good glug of olive oil to the tagine and let the onions and carrots simmer for about 5 minutes. Put the meat on top and add the vegetable stock. Close the lid and gently simmer for 1 hour.

Quarter the turnips and wash the spinach. Add the turnips and cook for 15 minutes. Add the spinach at the last minute. Season with salt, pepper and Ras el hanout. To finish, sprinkle with parsley.

TIP Serve with couscous.

5

VEGETARIAN

POTATO VEGETABLE TARTLETS

 Suitable for:
Closed barbecue, Outdoorchef, KitchenAid barbecue, Boretti, Weber, Green Egg, Grill Dome and Le Panyol.

SERVES 4

7 oz / 200 g spinach, from your own garden
if possible
4 potatoes
4 tsps of marinated tomatoes (see recipe for
carpaccio of smoked lamb fillet on p. 37)
7/8 cup / 2 dl cream

4 eggs
herbs for vegetables (of pepper, salt and nutmeg)

for the barbecue:
1 handful of herbs for the fire

Wash the spinach and slice into long strips. Cook the potatoes and mash them slightly with a fork. Combine with the pieces of tomato and the spinach. Combine the cream with the eggs and stir the mixture into the potatoes. Season with herbs for vegetables and pour the mixture into a muffin tin. Place under a closed lid barbecue for 30 minutes at 350 °F / 180 °C. Throw herbs for the fire onto the coals for a delicious, herby barbecue aroma.

TIP This is also a delicious side dish.

VEGETARIAN PIZZA WITH BELL PEPPERS FROM THE GARDEN

 Suitable for:
Le Panyol, but also for closed barbecue, Outdoorchef, Green Egg, Grill Dome, KitchenAid barbecue, Weber and Boretti with pizza stone.

SERVES 4

for the tomato sauce:
6 large organic tomatoes, from your own garden
2 shallots
olive oil
7/8 cup / 2 dl white wine
2 tsps of tomato puree
herbs for the barbecue
1 knifepoint of curry powder

for the pizza:
1 pre-made pizza crust
1 tomato, sliced into rounds

2 green bell peppers from the garden,
sliced into rings
some basil leaves
1 fresh buffalo mozzarella
6 oz / 150 g sovrano, grated
dried oregano
1 handful of arugula, from your
own garden if possible
olive oil

for the barbecue:
1 handful of olive pits

Cook the tomatoes for 6 minutes in a closed barbecue on a medium hot temperature (250 °F / 120 °C). Throw a handful of olive pits onto the coals for a smoky aroma. Slice the shallots finely and cook them in a generous dash of olive oil until translucent. Remove the skin from tomatoes and squeeze out the juice. Then add them to the shallots and fry for 5 minutes. Deglaze the pan with the white wine and tomato puree. Season with herbs for the barbecue and curry powder and place the pot in a closed barbecue for 30 minutes at 250 °F / 120 °C.

Coat the pizza crust with the tomato sauce and then place a few slices of tomato on top, followed by the rounds of bell pepper. Cover with the basil and slices of mozzarella. Sprinkle a little sovrano and oregano on top. Heat the ceramic pizza stone well or bake the pizza in a Le Panyol wood oven. Thrown some olive pits onto the bottom of the pizza oven or on to the grill for extra aroma. Bake the pizza at a high temperature of 570 to 660 °F / 300 to 350 °C until the pizza is golden brown. Finish with the fresh arugula and drizzle a little olive oil over the top.

```
Sovrano
This cheese from Lombardy is made in the same way as parmigiano and grana
padano, but from either cow or buffalo milk. Moreover, vegetable or non-
animal rennet is used. The cheese is matured for 18 months. Sovrano is
notable for its sweet flavor and hard, white rind. Weight: 66 to 88 lbs /
30 to 40 kg.
```

PARTY FORMULA

> 7 <

La fiesta total!

Nothing is more delicious than making a couple of fresh pizzas on the barbecue on a hot summer evening. Those who are lucky enough to have a Le Panyol wood oven shouldn't be in any doubt and will opt for this barbecue. You can make pizzas just as well on the pizza plate of any kind of closed barbecue, and the advantage is that each of your guests can choose what they would like to have on their pizza. It's also a great activity for kids, helping them to learn about new ingredients in a fun way. Make it into a relaxed party and put on some cheerful, summery tunes.

GRILLED BUTTERNUT SQUASH WITH A PAS-DE-BLUE-SAUCE AND ARUGULA

 Suitable for:
Closed and open barbecue, Buck, Bon Fire, Outdoorchef, KitchenAid barbecue, Boretti, Green Egg, Grill Dome.

SERVES 4

1 butternut squash
1 shallot
olive oil
1 dash of cognac
7/8 cup / 2 dl vegetable stock (see *The basics* on p. 27)
6 oz / 150 g Pas-de-Bleu
1/3 cup / 1 dl cream

herbs for vegetables (see *The basics* on p. 24)
1 handful of arugula
2-1/2 Tbs of walnuts, roasted and chopped

for the barbecue:
1 handful of herbs for the fire (see *The basics* on p. 24)

Peel the squash, cut it in half and remove the seeds. Cut into slices 3/16 in / 1 cm thick. Finely chop the shallot and fry until golden in olive oil. Deglaze the pan with the cognac. Add the vegetable stock and leave the cheese to melt in it. Then add the cream and blend with a handheld mixer. Rub the squash slices with olive oil and season with herbs for vegetables. Grill until al dente in a fish grill for about 6 minutes on a medium hot grill. Throw the herbs for the fire onto the coals for aroma. Serve the squash with the sauce, the arugula and the walnuts.

ROASTED SEASONAL VEGETABLES FROM THE GARDEN

Suitable for:
Closed and open barbecue, Buck, Bon Fire, Outdoorchef, KitchenAid barbecue, Boretti, Green Egg, Grill Dome.

SERVES 4

a mixture of parsnip, sweet potato, carrots, celery, red onions, kohlrabi
7/8 cup / 2 dl olive oil
herbs for vegetables (see *The basics* on p. 24)
1 bulb of garlic, cut through the middle
4 sprigs of thyme
4 sprigs of rosemary
juice of 1 lemon

2 tsps of maple syrup
2 tsps of spicy mustard
6 oz / 150 g capers
cumin seeds (optional)

for the barbecue:
herbs for the fire (see *The basics* on p. 24)

Slice the vegetables lengthwise. Put them in a bowl and rub liberally with olive oil. Season with herbs for vegetables. Place them in a wok topper (wok with holes) or on the grillplate, add the garlic and sprinkle over the finely chopped rosemary and thyme. Grill for 45 minutes over a medium hot barbecue. Regularly throw herbs for the fire on the grill. Make a sauce of the lemon juice, maple syrup, mustard and sliced capers. Serve the vegetables with the sauce and, if you like, with some toasted cumin seeds.

Grilled Jerusalem artichokes with Greek yoghurt sauce

GRILLED JERUSALEM ARTICHOKES WITH GREEK YOGHURT SAUCE

Suitable for:
Closed and open barbecue, Buck, Bon Fire, Outdoorchef, KitchenAid barbecue, Boretti, Green Egg, Grill Dome

SERVES 4

1.75 lbs / 800 g Jerusalem artichokes, from your own garden if possible
lemon water
herbs for vegetables (see *The basics* on p. 24)
1-1/4 cups / 3 dl olive oil (or herb marinade)
1 bunch of thyme
juice of 3 lemons

14 oz / 400 g small tomatoes, from your garden if possible
1/2 cucumber
1-1/2 cups / 300 g Greek yoghurt
1 bunch of fresh cilantro
pepper and salt
2 tsps of cumin seeds, roasted

Peel the Jerusalem artichokes with a vegetable peeler and slice them lengthwise into sections 3/16 in / 1 cm thick. Place them immediately into the lemon water to prevent them from turning brown. Remove them from the water and rub them with olive oil.

Season with herbs for vegetables, thyme and the lemon juice and roast them for 40 minutes on a grill over a medium hot barbecue (340 °F / 170 °C). Slice the tomatoes in half and place them on the grill for the final 5 minutes. Grate the cucumber into the yoghurt and season with the chopped cilantro, pepper, salt and cumin seeds. Serve the roasted Jerusalem artichokes with the yoghurt sauce.

POTATO TART WITH OREGANO AND LEAF LETTUCE

 Suitable for:
Closed barbecue, Outdoorchef, KitchenAid barbecue, Boretti, Weber, Green Egg,
Grill Dome and Le Panyol.

SERVES 4

1.1 lbs / 500 g small potatoes (Belle de Fontenay)
7 oz / 200 g small tomatoes, from your
garden if possible
olive oil
4 sprigs of fresh oregano, finely chopped
sea salt
ground pepper
2 Tbs of sugar
3 Tbs of butter oregano leaves, chopped

herbs for vegetables (see *The basics* on p. 24)
1 large onion
dried tomatoes
7 oz / 200 g testum con mosto (hard cheese
with rind)
2 sprigs of rosemary
1 sheet of ready-made pie dough
1 handful of fresh lettuce, from your
garden if possible

Cook the potatoes in their skins until al dente. Slice the tomatoes in half and place them on an oven tray with parchment paper. Sprinkle them with some olive oil and then the oregano, sea salt and pepper. Place in an oven at 230 °F / 110 °C for 1 hour to dry out.

Line an 8 in / 22 cm cake pan with baking paper. Place the sugar and the butter into a stainless-steel pan and heat it until you get a light caramel. Pour over the baking paper in the cake pan and shake gently from side to side until the bottom is fully covered. Sprinkle with chopped oregano leaves. Cut the potatoes into thick slices and lay them close together on top of the caramel. Season with herbs for vegetables. Cut the onion into thin rings and place on the potatoes. Gently place the dried tomatoes on top and then the slices of cheese on top of that until everything is covered. Top off with the sheet of pastry and ensure that 1 in / 3 cm of pastry hang over the cake pan on all sides. Prick it with a fork a few times and allow the tart to set in the refrigerator for a day.

On the day of the barbecue bake the tart for 40 minutes in a closed barbecue at 350 °F / 180 °C. Lay a plate on top of the tart and, in one quick movement, turn the tart over. Like a tarte tatin. Serve the potato tart with fresh lettuce.

STUFFED PIZZA WITH MUSHROOMS, TRUFFLE AND PECORINO

 Suitable for:
Le Panyol, closed barbecue, Outdoorchef, Green Egg, Grill Dome, Weber, KitchenAid barbecue, Boretti, with pizza stone

SERVES 4

2 red onions
1.33 lbs / 600 g mixture of wild of mushrooms
4 ready-made pizza crusts (uncooked)
7 oz / 200 g black olive tapenade
herbs for vegetables (see *The basics* on p. 24)

4 tsps of flat leaf parsley, chopped
4 tsps of sage, chopped
1 truffle
7 oz / 200 g pecorino, grated
1 pinch of flour

Slice the onions into thin rings. Rinse the mushrooms under cold water and dry them well. Lay out the pizza crusts and rub them with the olive tapenade. Divide the mushrooms across one half of each pizza crust, so that you'll still be able to fold them closed. Then add the onion rings and season with herbs for vegetables. Sprinkle them with the fresh chopped herbs and shred the truffle over the pizzas. Add the grated cheese and fold the pizzas closed. Sprinkle lightly with flour and bake for 10 minutes in a Le Panyol wood oven or in a closed barbecue on the pizza stone at 446 °F / 230 °C.

GRILLED YOUNG LEEKS FROM THE GARDEN WITH MARINATED BELL PEPPERS

 Suitable for:
Closed and open barbecue, Buck, Bon Fire, Outdoorchef, KitchenAid barbecue, Boretti, Green Egg, Grill Dome.

SERVES 4

20 small young leeks
olive oil
herbs for vegetables (see *The basics* on p. 24)
2 red bell peppers
5 cardamom pods
20 pink peppercorns
10 coriander seeds
1-1/4 cups / 3 dl water
7/8 cup / 2 dl cider vinegar
scant 1/2 cup / 80 g sugar

for the barbecue:
1 handful of herbs for the fire (see *The basics* on p. 24)

to serve:
fresh herbs of your choice
fresh flowers

Rub the leeks with olive oil and season with herbs for vegetables. Slice the peppers into 1/8 in / 5 mm strips. Toast the cardamom pods, peppercorns and coriander seeds and grind them fine with a mortar and pestle. Add the water, cider vinegar, ground herbs and sugar to a stainless-steel pan and heat. Add the pepper strips, bring to a boil then turn off the heat and leave to cool. Grill the leeks. Throw a handful of herbs for the fire onto the coals for an extra herby aroma. Serve with the marinated peppers, your choice of fresh herbs and some flowers.

Q-BAG WITH BABY ROOT VEGETABLES WITH CURLY ENDIVE HERB PESTO

 Suitable for:
Open barbecue, Bon Fire, Buck (or leave the top of the barbecue off)

SERVES 4

2.2 lbs / 1 kg baby root vegetables, e.g. baby
beetroot, young turnips, young carrots
2 quarts / 2 liters of chicken stock

for the pesto:
7 oz / 200 g curly endive
1/2 cup / 50 g walnuts
1/2 cup / 50 g hazelnuts
3 cloves of garlic
4 tsps of sovrano, grated

juice of 1 lemon
150 ml olive oil
2 Tbs of nut oil
pepper
Maldon salt

to serve:
herbs for vegetables (see *The basics* on p. 22)
3-1/3 cups / 8 dl chicken stock

Wash the vegetables thoroughly, leaving them in their skins. Cook them in the chicken stock. Place all of the ingredients for the pesto into a blender and mix until you have a green puree, making sure it does not become too fine. Place the vegetables in a bowl and combine with the pesto. Season with herbs for vegetables and divide across four Q-bags. Pour a quarter of the chicken stock into each Q-bag and fold twice to close. Place them on a hot grill for 10 minutes.

VEGETABLE TART WITH RICOTTA AND FRESH GARDEN HERBS

 Suitable for:
Closed barbecue, Outdoorchef, Le Panyol, Green Egg, Grill Dome, KitchenAid barbecue, Weber, Boretti

 TIP I make the tart with zucchini, pumpkin, bell peppers, tomatoes, onions and eggplants from the garden, but in principle you can make this tart with any vegetables you like.

SERVES 4

a mixture of vegetables of your choice
olive oil
herbs for vegetables (see *The basics* on p. 24)
Herbes de Provence
10.5 oz / 300 g ready-made puff pastry
9 oz / 250 g ricotta
2 free range eggs
7/8 cup / 2 dl cream
3 fresh bay leaves
lemon thyme

tarragon
sage
oregano
basil
chives
salt and pepper

for the barbecue:
1 handful of olive pits

Grill the bell peppers until they are blackened and then place them in a plastic bag for 20 minutes to make them easy to peel. Slice the vegetables, except the tomatoes, into large chunks 3/4 in / 2 cm in size, place them in a bowl and rub them with olive oil and herbs for vegetables. Toss some of the Herbes de Provence over them and grill until al dente on a grill in a closed barbecue. Throw the olive pits onto the coals for extra aroma.

Grease a cake pan with oil, line with baking paper and roll the pastry into the pan. You should leave 1 in / 3 cm of pastry hanging over the sides. Prick the bottom of the pastry with a fork and bake for 20 minutes at 320 °F / 160 °C. Take the cake pan off of the barbecue and spread the grilled vegetables over the tart. Spread the ricotta over the vegetables, Slice the tomatoes in half and place them cut side up on top of the vegetables. Beat the eggs with the cream and sprinkle in the finely chopped fresh herbs. Season with salt and pepper and pour the mixture over the vegetables. Bake the tart for 40 minutes in a closed barbecue at 340 °F / 170 °C. Before taking the tart out, check to make sure it's firm enough.

VEGETABLE DISH GRILLED IN A LA TERRA POT

 Suitable for:
Closed barbecue, KitchenAid barbecue, Weber...

SERVES 4

4.4 lbs / 2 kg seasonal vegetables such as carrots,
turnips, onions, kohlrabi, zucchini, peppers
olive oil
herbs for vegetables (see *The basics* on p. 24)
thyme
bay leaf
rosemary
savory

7/8 cup / 2 dl red wine
7/8 cup / 2 dl vegetable stock
4 tsp Thai basil, chopped
4 tsp sesame seeds, toasted

for the barbecue:
1 handful of herbs for the fire (see *The basics* on p. 24)

Clean the vegetables and slice into large, 1 in / 3 cm pieces. Place the La Terra-pot on the grill and add a generous dash of olive oil. Cook the vegetables for 10 minutes, season with herbs for vegetables and thyme, bay leaf, rosemary and savory. Deglaze with the red wine and the vegetable stock. Leave to simmer for another 15 minutes with the lid on. Throw the herbs for the fire onto the coals for a spicy aroma. Finish with the basil and the sesame seeds. You'll see that the pot will exude its aroma.

```
The La Terra pot
This organic piece of culinary ceramic is made in Colombia in the small village
of La Chamba. It's made by hand from two types of clay according to an age-old
tradition, on the banks of the River Magdalen. This traditional pottery differs
from industrially made items due to being completely hand-made and being only of
natural materials. Every pot or dish is made smooth using a tigers-eye
burnishing stone, and is blackened and glazed naturally. The La Terra-ceramic
range is safe for all kinds of heat (excluding induction ovens) and can even be
used in the oven, microwave and dishwasher.
http://delaterraconcepts.com/products
```

6

DESSERTS

PUMPKIN WITH VANILLA GINGER CREAM

Suitable for:
Closed barbecue, Outdoorchef, Le Panyol, Green Egg, Grill Dome, KitchenAid barbecue, Weber, Boretti...

SERVES 4

1 small pumpkin
6 eggs
1/2 cup / 100 g cane sugar
2/3 cups / 150 ml cream

1 vanilla pod
1 knifepoint of ground ginger
1 knifepoint of ground cinnamon

Slice off the top of the pumpkin and remove the seeds. Beat the eggs with the sugar and add the cream. Slice the vanilla pod along the center, remove the inside with a knife and add this to the egg mixture along with the ginger and cinnamon. Fill the pumpkin with the mixture, replace the top, and bake for an hour and a half in a closed barbecue at 210 °F / 100 °C.

grilled pineapple

GRILLED PINEAPPLE

Suitable for:
Closed barbecue, Outdoorchef, Boretti, KitchenAid barbecue, Green Egg, Grill Dome, Le Panyol.

SERVES 4

2/3 cup / 150 ml water
1.7 oz / 50 g instant marinade for dessert

1 pineapple
ice cream of your choice

Combine the water and the instant marinade in a bowl. Leave the pineapple whole, but make a couple of holes underneath it. Place the pineapple in a plastic bag while you inject the marinade. Place the pineapple in a closed barbecue for 1 hour. Slice into 1/2 in / 1 cm rounds and serve with a scoop of ice-cream.

TIP On an open barbecue, first slice the pineapple into rounds and then grill. You can also mix a few fresh mint leaves into the marinade and pass the mixture through a sieve before injecting the pineapple with the marinade.

> GRILLED FIGS

 Suitable for:
Closed barbecue, Outdoorchef, Le Panyol, KitchenAid barbecue, Green Egg,
Grill Dome, Weber, Boretti.

SERVES 4
for the sauce:
1 cup / 2.5 dl coconut milk
3 egg yolks
1/3 cup / 60 g vanilla sugar
1 bag of mint tea

for the figs:
1.7 oz / 50 g instant marinade for dessert
2/3 cup / 150 ml water
12 ripe figs

to serve:
7/8 cup / 2 dl maple syrup
4 scoops of vanilla ice cream
2 Tbs of coconut flakes

for the barbecue:
herbs for the fire (see *The basics* on p. 24)

First make the sauce. Take 4 tsps of the coconut milk and beat the egg yolks into it. Heat the rest of the coconut milk with the vanilla sugar and leave the teabag to infuse in it. Remove the stainless-steel pan from the heat and remove the teabag. Stir into the lightly beaten eggs yolks and place it back over low heat for one minute. Stir the sauce until it thickens a little, but make sure that the sauce does not heat above 176 °F / 80 °C. Then pour immediately into a cold bowl and leave to cool.

Combine the instant marinade with the water and baste the figs with this. Slice the figs in half and place them cut side up above the embers of the barbecue for around 8 minutes, depending on how ripe the fruits are. Throw some herbs for the fire onto the coals for a typical barbecue flavor and to refresh the fire a little. Dress the figs on a plate with a scoop of ice-cream and some maple syrup. Finish with some coconut flakes.

 If you cannot find maple syrup, you can also use golden syrup or heated pear
or apple syrup.

PINEAPPLE WITH MINT MARINADE AND SABAYON OF TIMMERMANS CHERRY BEER

 Suitable for:
Closed barbecue, Outdoorchef, Le Panyol, KitchenAid barbecue, Green Egg, Grill Dome, Weber, Boretti...

SERVES 4
1 large pineapple
mint marinade (see *The basics* on p. 27)

for the sabayon:
4 egg yolks
1 vanilla pod
1/2 cup / 140 ml Timmermans cherry beer
1/2 cup / 100 g cane sugar

First place the pineapple into a plastic bag and inject it with the mint marinade. Place it in a closed barbecue for 1 hour at 350 °F / 180 °C. Now make the sabayon. Put the egg yolks into a stainless-steel pan, slice the vanilla pod in half and scrape out the inside. Add this to the egg yolks, along with the beer and the sugar. Beat the mixture over a low heat until foaming. The eggs should not be heated above 179 °F / 82 °C or you'll end up with a sweet omelet. Slice the pineapple and serve with the sabayon.

PARTY FORMULA

> 8 <

Barbecue for kids

Fire appeals to people of all ages. If you are expecting lots of children, there's nothing better than filling a huge fire basket with big logs, like a bonfire (see photo). Spread a couple of big sheets out on the ground, throw a few cushions on top and adorn the garden and the trees with decorations of your choosing. It's the perfect moment to have a summer picnic and for the children to try all kinds of little, special and easy foods. For dessert, they could stick pieces of nougat on the end of wooden skewers and hold them over the fire like marshmallows until they are toasted. They'll talk about it for years to come!

> APPLE TART MADE ON THE BARBECUE

 Suitable for:
Closed barbecue, Outdoorchef, Le Panyol, KitchenAid barbecue, Green Egg, Grill Dome, Weber, Boretti...

SERVES 4

for the pastry:
7/8 cup / 100 g flour
1 cup / 100 g ground almonds
1/2 cup / 100 g butter
1 pinch Chinese five spice powder
1/2 cup / 100 g lightly packed brown sugar

for the puree of lemon:
2 cups / 5 dl milk
zest of 3 lemons
4 egg yolks
1/2 cup / 100 g sugar
1/2 cup / 60 g flour

to serve:
olive oil
3 apples, sliced

Combine the flour, ground almonds, softened butter, Chinese five spice powder and the brown sugar in a dish and leave to rest for 1 hour. Heat the milk with the lemon zest. Combine the egg yolks with the sugar and flour. Take the milk off the heat and stir in the eggs. Place over low heat and stir until you get a thick puree.

Roll out the pastry and grease a baking tin with a little oil. Place the pastry into it and pour the puree over it. Cover with the sliced apple. Place the tart in a closed barbecue for 30 minutes at 350 °F / 180 °C.

```
Chinese five spice powder
This Chinese herb mixture is made up of
cinnamon, star anise, pepper, fennel and
clove. It contains the five taste groups:
sweet, salt, bitter, sour and umami. This herb
mixture has 'dominant' flavor and should
therefore be used sparingly.
```

GRILLED PEARS FROM THE GARDEN WITH CHOCOLATE SABAYON

Suitable for:
Open and closed barbecue, Buck, Bon Fire, Outdoorchef, KitchenAid barbecue, Weber, Boretti, Green Egg, Grill Dome

SERVES 4

2 cups / 0.5 liters of red wine
2 cups / 0.5 liters of Timmermans raspberry beer
4 cloves
2 cinnamon sticks
3/4 cup / 150 g sugar
1 vanilla pod
4 large pears

for the sabayon:
3 egg yolks
scant 1/2 cup / 100 g Timmermans raspberry beer
1/3 cup / 75 g sugar
4 tsps of cocoa powder

to serve:
raspberries
some sweet herbs from the garden such
as basil or mint

Heat the wine and the beer with the cloves, the cinnamon sticks, the sugar and the open vanilla pod and allow to infuse for 10 minutes. In the meantime, peel the pears and then cook them in this liquid for 30 minutes until they are al dente. Allow them to cool in the liquid. Put the egg yolks, beer, sugar and cocoa powder in a stainless-steel pan and until foamy. Grill the pears for 6 minutes on a hot barbecue and serve with some fresh raspberries, sweet herbs and the sabayon.

Q-bag with seasonal fruit
and chocolate pesto

Q-BAG WITH SEASONAL FRUIT AND CHOCOLATE PESTO

 Suitable for:
Open barbecue, Bon Fire, Buck (or leave the top off).

SERVES 4

for the pesto:
the inside of 1 vanilla pod
scant 1/2 cup / 60 g cashew nuts
2 tsps of cocoa
4 tsps ground cocoa beans
1-1/8 cups / 100 g mint
1/4 cup / 60 ml coconut oil
1/3 cup / 1 dl maple syrup
2 tsps of olive oil

for the fruit:
1.75 lbs / 800 g fruit, e.g. apples, pears or pineapple
1-3/4 cups / 4 dl almond milk

for the barbecue:
4 Q-bags

Place all of the ingredients for the pesto into a blender and mix to a pesto consistency. Peel the fruit and slice. Combine the pesto with the fruit. Fill the Q-bags with this and pour a quarter of the almond milk into each Q-bag. Fold twice to close and place on an open grill for around 15 minutes. You will be able to see when the fruit's ready by looking through the Q-bag window.

`TIP` When you serve this, sprinkle a handful of toasted almonds over the fruit.

> GRILLED STRAWBERRIES, STRAWBERRY JUICE AND PUREE OF BASIL

 Suitable for:
Open barbecue, Bon Fire, Buck (or leave the lid off).

SERVES 4
4.5 lbs / 2 kg sweet strawberries
2.2 lbs / 1 kg nice big strawberries

for the puree:
2 eggs
1/8 cup / 30 g lemon juice
3 Tbs / 35 g sugar
1 leaf of gelatin, soaked in water
1 cup / 25 g basil leaves
scant 1/4 cup / 50 g ice-cold butter

to serve:
ground black pepper

for the barbecue:
1 handful of herbs for the fire (see *The basics* on p. 24)

Grill the sweet strawberries briefly in a wok topper (wok with holes) or on a grill plate. Throw the herbs for the fire onto the coals for a spicy aroma. Place the strawberries into a sieve and allow to drain for 24 hours. Save the juice.

Grill the big strawberries for 3 minutes over a hot barbecue. Warm the eggs, the lemon juice and the sugar for 7 minutes in a pan at 176 °F / 80 °C and then for a further minute at 176 °F / 90 °C. Add the gelatin and then cool the pan over ice until it reaches 113 °F / 45 °C. Mix it with the basil leaves. Now, bit by bit, add the ice-cold butter and mix until you have a puree. Allow the mixture to harden in the refrigerator. Pour a base of the strawberry juice into deep bowls, place the strawberries into these and add a spoonful or two of basil puree on top. Finish with a little black pepper.

TIP You can easily prepare the strawberry juice and the basil puree a day or two in advance.

STUFFED PEARS WITH REAL CUBERDON CANDIES AND ALMONDS

Suitable for:
Closed barbecue, Outdoorchef, Le Panyol, Green Egg, KitchenAid barbecue, Grill Dome, Weber, Boretti.

SERVES 4

4 nice pears
4 cuberdon candies
2 tsps of almond slivers, toasted

2 tsps of fresh mint, chopped
4 raspberries
ice cream of your choice

Slice the tops off of the pears, remove the core and create a hollow inside. Slice the cuberdon candies and combine with the almond slivers and the mint. Place one raspberry into each pear. Spoon the cuberdon mixture into the pears and put the tops back on. Grill the pears for 15 to 20 minutes in a closed barbecue. Serve with a scoop of ice cream.

> RED FRUIT WITH BASIL UNDER A CUBERDON CANDY CRUMBLE

 Suitable for:
Closed and open barbecue, Buck, Bon Fire, Outdoorchef, KitchenAid barbecue, Weber, Boretti, Green Egg, Grill Dome.

SERVES 4

for the crumble:
3/4 cup / 90 g flour
2.25 oz / 65 g cuberdon candy crunch
1/3 cup / 75 g soft butter at room temperature
a pinch of salt

for the fruit:
7/8 cup / 125 g blackberries
7/8 cup / 125 g raspberries
7/8 cup / 125 g strawberries
7/8 cup / 125 g blueberries
5 fresh basil leaves, chopped
2 cuberdon candies
2 tsps of old port
1 lemon

Combine everything for the crumble in a bowl.

Place the fruit in a fireproof bowl. Sprinkle it with the chopped basil, place the cuberdon candies in among the fruit and sprinkle with a little port. Grate the zest of the lemon over the top and sprinkle the crumble over the fruit. Place into a closed barbecue for 20 minutes at 392 °F / 200 °C.

GROWING YOUR OWN
VEGETABLES, FRUIT AND HERBS

> GROWING YOUR OWN VEGETABLES, FRUIT AND HERBS

Over the course of this book you may have noticed that I have something of a passion for home-grown, fresh ingredients. I do of course understand that not everyone has such an extensive garden as the one we've been able to create at Elckerlijc Farm, but it's possible to create a lovely garden in just a small area and without too much effort. Admit it: fresh cauliflower or lettuce from the garden has such a delicious taste! Below are a few notes about types of fruit and vegetables that are relatively easy to grow, if you have a garden. If you don't have a garden, you can always source fresh ingredients for your barbecue from your local grocery or produce stand. I also list my favorite types of fruit for the barbecue and an overview of a basic herb garden. Herbs don't take up much space and are something that everyone can grow. Your guests will thank you for it!

A. The vegetable garden

Below is a concise overview of vegetables that you can grow yourself. Most vegetables require at least a little work and time, but really it's all about planning a weekly routine. For example, taking a minute or two each day to remove any new weeds is an important step in looking after your crop. And of course, when necessary, the plants require water. The results are absolutely worth the effort, especially if you are planning a barbecue and want to treat your guests to the most delicious ingredients. I have divided up the vegetables based on the seasons in which they can be harvested. The following descriptions give an overview of the preparation, sowing times, maintenance and harvesting. There are also a few warnings.

Vegetable garden ABC

Mounding: Placing soil against the bottom or a plant into order to anchor it in place or to protect it.

Bed: Part of the garden intended for growing a specific crop.

Protective foil: This protects the smaller, more vulnerable plants in winter. It's a very thin, light type of plastic wrap. Spread it out across the vegetables and keep it in place using stones so that the ends do not come undone.

Compost: This digested organic material (such as garden and vegetable waste) is used to improve the soil.

Pregrowth: This indicates the premature production of flowers and seeds, which can sometimes make vegetables inedible.

An annual: A plant with a life cycle of only one year.

Lime composting: Composting the soil to enrich it with calcium..

Mulch: This is covering layer made up of various materials (straw, grass cuttings, cocoa pods, etc.), intended to protect plants from the cold or to absorb moisture.

Plastic tunnels: Also known as cold frames or row covers, they're often used to grow lettuce, for example. To make one, you will need to put thin plastic sheeting (polyethylene foil protects against UV rays) over semi-circular frames of metal or plastic. The entire thing must be properly fixed to the ground with string and sticks.

A biennial: A plant with a life cycle of two years.

Thinning: This is the process of removing the weakest seedlings in order to encourage the growth of stronger plants.

Weeding: Weeds are the biggest problem in the garden. Make sure that you weed your garden regularly, preferably for a few minutes everyday in order to remove all of the young weeds.

Seed hole: This is a small hole into which many seeds are placed and then covered with soil. It's advisable with certain vegetables to sow multiple seeds, such as with pumpkin, and to only keep the strongest plant.

Types of soil

Vegetables require perfectly balanced soil. Some types of soil require a bit of improvement. An overview:

Sandy soil: This soil crumbles easily and dries out quickly. In the summertime you need to water it regularly. Enrich it often with peat (1.25 lbs/yd^2 or 500 g/m^2), fertilizer or compost (6.75 lbs/yd^2 or 3 kg/m^2).

Clay based soil: This soil is sticky, heats slowly in the springtime and is not easy to plow. Enrich it with turf, a little sand and fine lime.

Compost rich soil: This soil contains vegetable waste and retains water well. Enrich it now and then with lime.

Potassium-rich soil: This soil is easily permeable, absorbs heat quickly in the springtime, but is not suitable for most types of vegetables. Therefore, add fertilizer or compost (6.75 lbs/yd^2 or 3 kg/m^2) regularly.

Seasonal overview

Spring

All types of salad: These annual plants do well in most types of soil, but avoid overly salty or acidic soil. Enrich the earth when plowing with potassium-rich compost and water regularly. *Sow* from February to September under a plastic tunnel. Make rows of seeds that are 12 to 15 in or 30 to 40 cm apart. *Maintain* by regularly hoeing the soil to make it lighter. Water, but not on the salad leaves or they'll rot. *Pick* the salad preferably in the morning and before it goes to seed. Salad does not keep after being picked and should be eaten quickly. You can *keep* it for around 24 hours in the vegetable tray of a refrigerator if you wrap it in saran wrap.

Tomatoes: These annuals cannot take the cold and do best in well-composted soil. *Sow* in April. Germinate the seed for 24 hours in a container with water and then transfer to a plant pot placed by the window. As soon as the seedlings appear, plant the strongest ones out into soil trays. Plant them out into the garden from the beginning of May, 15 in or 40 cm apart. Or you could just buy young plants. *Maintain* by digging small holes at the base of every plant and watering regularly. *Pick* the tomatoes once they have a nice red color.

Cauliflower: This vegetable cannot take extremes or heat or cold. Add well-decomposed manure or compost to the soil in winter. *Sow* from January in a heated greenhouse or from April to June in the garden. Give the plant time to grow and water every now and then. *Maintain* by regularly hoeing the ground around the plants. *Pick* five to eight months from sowing and once the crop is properly visible.

Zucchini: This vegetable is highly sensitive to frost and requires a sunny spot that heats up quickly. Enrich the soil prior to sowing with vegetable mulch and a little fertilizer or compost. During the growth period, water with a liquid fertilizer. *Sow* from April or May: place three or four seeds into each hole. Keep them 3 ft or 1 m apart. Once the seedlings have three or four leaves, keep the nicest one and remove the others. *Maintain* by hoeing the

area around the plants and weeding. Water regularly at the base of the plant. *Pick* them before they are ripe, as this encourages the production of the female flowers, the only flowers that produce fruit. *Harvest* from June. Zucchinis can be *kept* for four to five days in a cool, dry place. When sliced into rounds and blanched, they will keep well in the freezer.

Eggplant: This vegetable requires lots of heat and good quality soil, rich in organic materials (e.g., composted in the previous year with vegetable mulch.) *Sow* the seeds in April and May in pots, 1.25 in or 3 cm apart and press them 3/4 in or 2 cm into the soil. Place them in an environment with a temperature around 68 °F or 20 °C and water regularly. Once they have five leaves, the seedlings can be transferred into seed trays and placed into the greenhouse or cold-frame. You can also buy young plants from a garden centre. Plant them out in May, in a cold greenhouse, about 18 in or 50 cm apart. *Maintain* them by watering them via a hole at the base of the plant. Every two weeks add a potassium-rich fertilizer to their water. Limit the number of fruit to four to six per plant. *Harvest* in August and September. You can *keep* eggplant for a maximum of one week in the vegetable tray of the refrigerator.

Bell pepper: Bell peppers require lots of heat and do well in normal soil that is rich in organic materials. *Sow* into pot with digested compost in February-March. Make the soil wet and place a glass plate on top of the pot. Place the pot on a radiator, in the light. As soon as the seedlings appear, remove the glass plate during the daytime. Place them in the garden at the end of May beginning of July, keeping them 18 in or 50 cm apart, both plants and rows. *Maintain* by watering often and placing roof tiles around the plant to retain the heat of sun for as long as possible. Watch out for mildew and if you need to use a special anti-mildew solution. *Harvest* at the end of July or at the first sign of frost. Always pick the fruit with its stem attached.

Also this season:
Radishes, spring onions, endive, all types of beans.

Summer

Leaf lettuce: As with all types of lettuce (see Spring), this vegetable does well in most types of soil, apart from those that are particularly salty or acidic. Enrich the soil with potassium-rich fertilizer and add soil regularly. To encourage growth, add oxygen rich fertilizer a couple of times. *Sow* from February to September under a plastic tunnel. Create rows 12 to 15 in or 30 to 40 cm apart. Press the seeds lightly into the soil and keep the soil moist. As soon as the seedlings have four or five leaves, thin them out until the remaining plants are 10 in or 25 cm apart. You can also just buy seed-

lings and sow straight into the garden. *Maintain* by hoeing the soil around the plants to make it lighter. Water the plants, but do not get the leaves wet or they'll rot. Watch out for slugs. Harvest from April to November. Pick in the morning, and preferably before the lettuce goes to seed. Lettuce does not keep for long. Wrapped in saran wrap, it can be *kept* for 24 hours in the vegetable tray of the refrigerator.

Carrot: This is a perennial plant that likes a moist and moderate climate. It does well in soil that's deeply plowed and which is rich in organic materials. Enrich the soil when plowing in the autumn with well-decomposed manure or compost and in the spring-time add nitrogen-rich fertilizer. *Sow* from February to July. Create holes 10 in or 25 cm deep, 15 in or 30 cm apart. Remove all stone, roots and waste. Distribute the seeds. Press soil on top, fluff the rows using the back of a rake and spread everything. Thin the seedlings and maintain a distance between the plants of 3 to 4 in or 8 to 10 cm. *Maintain* by regularly watering the plants and hoeing. Watch out for black fly. Two weeks prior to sowing, add some insecticide pellets to the soil. In the event of a serious frost, cover with a layer of fallen leaves or turf. *Harvest* in January and February and from May to December. Pull the carrots from the soil on a dry day and leave them to dry for two or three days on the ground.

Cucumber: This annual prefers light, nutritious soil that is rich in organic materials and cannot take extreme heat or cold. Enrich the soil when plowing with well-decomposed manure or compost and with potassium-rich fertilizer. *Sow* in March and April. Dig seed holes 1.5 to 2 in or 4 to 5 cm deep, 32 in or 80 cm apart. Keep rows 3 ft or 1 meter apart. Place three or four seeds into each hole. Once the seedlings have three or four leaves, leave the one with the best leaves and remove the rest. *Maintain* by watering well and before the hottest hour of day. Don't allow the leaves to become too wet. Watch out for slugs. *Harvest* in August and September. Do not *store* at room temperature, as they will quickly dry out. Place them in the refrigerator, but do not leave them for more than five days.

Onion: Onions like light, solid soil without too much compost. Enrich the soil with low CO_2 fertilizer. *Sow* colored types in March, in rows 8 in or 20 cm apart. White onions are sown in the second half of August and planted until the end of September. Plant the bulbs no deeper than 1 to 1.5 in or 2 to 3 cm with the point facing up and cover with ½ in or 1 cm of soil. Thin them out until 3 in or 8 cm apart. *Maintain* by regular hoeing. Do not water the plants, except during a long period of drought. *Harvest* from April to June or from July to September, depending on the type. Do this on a dry day and leave the onions to dry out on the ground for three or

179

four days. *Store* them in a cool, well ventilated place, in cupboards or hang up in bunches. Check them regularly for mold.

Patisson-pumpkin: This pumpkin-like fruit is flat, round and serrated and has gigantic leaves and yellow flowers. Patisson is eaten in the same way as zucchini. The plant requires rich soil with well-decomposed manure or compost and nitrogen-rich mulch. *Sow* in mid April. Place two or three seeds in holes full of soil, peat, fertilizer and compost. Thin the seedlings out and keep only the best plants. Bed them out in May, after the last freeze, 3 ft or 1 meter apart. *Maintain* through regular watering; this plant requires a great deal of water. Cover the base with a 2.75 to 3 in or 7 to 8 cm thick layer of mulch to keep the soil nutrient rich. *Harvest* in August-September. Press your nail into the fruit, if you can, then it's ripe. You can *store* the fruit for a few weeks in a cool, well ventilated place.

Fennel: Fennel is delicious raw and grated, steamed or boiled. Fennel cannot handle frost or extreme heat and enjoys a sunny spot. Enrich the soil when plowing with well-decomposed manure or compost and in the summertime add some potassium-rich, fast-acting mulch a few times. *Sow* in March under glass and plant out after the last frost. Keep plants 8 in or 20 cm apart in trenches 16 in or 40 cm apart. Cold weather means that it's safer to buy plants in May and then plant them out. *Maintain* by hoe-

ing the trenches closed and watering sufficiently. Watch out for slugs. *Harvest* in August and September; use a trowel or do this by hand if the soil is not too heavy. You can *keep* fennel bulbs in the refrigerator for a week.

Spinach: Delicious boiled, but also raw in a salad. The plant requires nutritious soil. Plant in the same spot only once every four years. The vegetable cannot handle extreme drought. Spinach also requires a great deal of fertilization: start with a well-decomposed manure or compost in the autumn and winter. Add a potassium-rich fertilizer and fast acting nitrogen-rich fertilizer once the seedlings are 1.5 to 2 in or 4 to 5 cm high. *Sow* in March-April at the earliest or better still from mid-August to the end of September, two or three times. Sow in rows 12 in or 30 cm apart. Thin the seedlings out until they are 4 in or 10 cm apart. *Maintain:* hoe the soil twice, to prevent pre-growth. Watch out for mildew. *Harvest* in March-April or in October-November, depending on when you've sown. Regularly pick the leaves once they are 3 to 4 in or 8 to 10 cm long. You can *store* spinach in the refrigerator for just two days, in an open bag. You can also freeze it quite easily.

Also this season:
tomatoes, chard, beans, bell peppers.

Autumn

Kohlrabi: Delicious raw sliced or grated, in soups or as a side dish. Kohlrabi likes low temperatures and is resistant to cold. The plant requires a moderate fertilizer (4.5 lbs/yd^2 or 2 kg/m^2 well-decomposed manure). *Sow* from March to June for a harvest from May to November. You can also sow at the start of September for winter harvesting. Do place a plastic tunnel over it, which you can remove in the daytime. Plant the seedlings and thin them out to 10 in or 25 cm apart and between the rows. *Maintenance:* water regularly. Watch out for slugs. *Harvest* two months after sowing. *Store* kohlrabi two per plastic bag with hole in it and place in the refrigerator. They will be fine for up to three days. You can freeze a batch of them after first slicing and blanching them. In winter they can be kept in a cool place.

Broccoli rabe: Also known as rapini is a vegetable popular in Italy. It's a turnip-like plant harvested for its flower and leaves. Rapini is stir fried or boiled and combined with garlic, onion and tomato. It has a spicy and slightly bitter taste. Rapini is an easy, low maintenance vegetable; normal composting is usually enough. *Sow* rapini from mid-March in good weather. Sow in a row and then thin out later. Seed germination is easy. It will need to be thinned out in order to get strong plants with a good flower head. *Maintain:* watch out for weeds in the rows and, as said, thin out to get the most flavorful leaves. *Harvest*: depending on the growth, the plant can be harvested four to six weeks later. The bottom part of the stalk should not be picked, as it will hopefully produce more leaves. Rapini does not *keep* for very long.

Butternut squash: Squash is possibly the easiest plant in the garden. The butternut is known for its soft, nutty flavor. Squash can be grown in almost any type of soil, but the best is sandy-loam and clay soils as pumpkins from these types of soil can be stored for longer than pumpkins grown in well-drained sandy soils. The soil in which pumpkins are grown must be well watered. *Sow* in May, in a greenhouse or under glass, as long as the minimum temperature is 54 °F / 12 °C. Place two or three seeds in each hole filled with compost. Thin the seedlings out once they have four leaves and plant them out into the soil in May. Keep 20 to 45 in or 50 to 120 cm apart. *Maintain*: mulch the plants regularly and water often. Watch out for mildew. *Harvest*: six months from sowing, in September-October. Pumpkins can be *stored* for months in a well-ventilated place at a temperature from 50 to 60°F / 10 to 20 °C.

Beetroot: This vegetable requires a great deal of fertilizer. Add well-decomposed manure to the soil in the autumn. And spread a potassium-rich fertilizer

two weeks prior to sowing. *Sow* from March to the end of June, 16 in or 40 cm apart, preferably in seed holes. Place four to five seeds in each hole, 8 in or 20 cm apart. Thin out and leave the healthiest plants in place. *Maintain*: hoe around the beetroot. Decontaminate the soil before sowing with insecticide pellets to prevent beetroot flies. *Harvest* from July to November. Beetroot can be *stored* for three to four days in the vegetable tray of the refrigerator in an air-tight container. You can also slice into rounds and store in the freezer for some months.

Turnip: Delicious boiled or steamed. Use normal fertilizer and a little fast-acting, nitrogen-rich fertilizer at the start of the growing process. The plant likes a moist climate, in not too deep and clay-based soil. *Sow*: depending on what it says on the seed packet, in February (under glass), in April (in soil bed) or in July-August. Thin out to 4 in or 10 cm apart with 12 in or 30 cm between rows. *Maintain*: water regularly. Watch out for clack fly and cabbage fly (there are special insecticides you can get to treat this). *Harvest* three months from sowing, between April and December. *Store*: turnips with no leaves can be stored for a week in the vegetable tray of the refrigerator. To keep longer, store them in the cellar in a container filled with sand.

Also this season:
leaf lettuce, lambs' lettuce, fennel, mini radishes (radishes

grown under a plastic tunnel make a nice garnish).

Winter

Brussels sprouts: These vegetables have a strong, long branch that ends in a bunch of large leaves with 25 to 70 miniature cabbages on it. If not harvested, it would become a useful, flowering sprig. In principle, any type of soil is suitable, but avoid soil that is overly acidic or too rich. It's enough to enrich once with fast-acting fertilizer, three to four weeks before sowing. *Sow* from the end of March to the start of May in rows. Plant the seedlings out a month later, 24 in or 60 cm apart. *Maintain*: watch out for mildew, a disease that covers plants with a white mold. Prevent this with sulfur. *Harvest* in January-February and November-December. Unwashed sprouts can be stored for a week in the vegetable tray. You can also blanch them for a few minutes and then *store* them in the freezer.

Winter radish: Only the root of this pant, with its rough skin, is edible and has a strong flavor. Delicious raw in salads or boiled like turnips. Winter radish is not a demanding plant, but requires a rich, light soil and a sunny spot. Enrich the soil beforehand with well-decomposed manure or compost. *Sow* in June-July. Place the seeds in the soil, 12 in or 30 cm apart, at a depth of 1.5 in or 3 to 4 cm. Thin the seedlings out until they are 6 in or 15 cm apart. *Maintain*: water the plants well. Keep the soil nutrient rich by adding mulch. Watch out for slugs and snails. *Store*: winter radish should be eaten soon after harvesting. You can store them for four or five days in the vegetable tray of the refrigerator or for three months in the cellar, in a container full of sand.

Cress: Cress can be grown easily year round at home. The seeds germinate quickly and the sprouts can be harvested after just a week. All you need is some gauze and a glass dish. *Sow*: soak a teaspoon full of cress seeds for 10 minutes. Then spread the soaked seeds out evenly over the gauze. Place the dish with the gauze in the sunshine (appx. 64 °F / 18 °C) and in the light (in the windowsill.) Leave the shoots to enjoy the sun, turning the dish daily. *Maintain*: spray with water often to prevent drying out. After just a few days, the shoots will begin to appear through the gauze, which you can clean from underneath daily. You can do this by lifting up the gauze and holding the underside of it under a lukewarm tap. *Harvest* as soon as the first leaves appear. You can best do this with a sharp knife or a pair of scissors. Cress germinates after a day and can be eaten from a week to two weeks from sowing. The sooner your harvest cress, the gentler the taste will be. You can also *store* it in the refrigerator for a few days. Cress loses its flavor once the plant dries out, which is why it's only eaten fresh.

Winter purslane: This is a rather bitter, spicy vegetable with heavy leaves that does well in constantly moist types of soil, preferably a sandy soil that is kept quite wet. *Sow*: it's usual to sow in August. If the soil temperature is still too high, germination will take longer. The seeds of winter purslane are small, but by mixing the seeds with fine sand it becomes easier to sow them in a more evenly dispersed way. After sowing, you do not have to cover the seeds with soil; it's enough to press lightly on them. Plant in rows of 8 in or 20 cm. *Maintain*: the plants need no fertilizer and only need to be covered in the event of a hard frost. *Harvest*: from late autumn to the end of the winter.

Pick from the outside and leave the center, this will produce new leaves and a new crop may follow.

Black salsify: This plant with pointed leaves has thick roots with a black skin that is edible. The young leaves are delicious, eaten raw in a salad. The plant requires sun, sandy and nutritious soil and likes to be planted deep. Enrich the soil in the autumn with well-decomposed manure or compost and in the springtime add fast-acting nitrogen-rich fertilizer. *Sow* in March-April in rows 10 in or 25 cm apart. Cover the seeds with .75 in or 2 cm of soil and press down well. Give them a little water. Thin the seedlings out until 3 in or 8 cm apart. This vegetable can stay in the ground for up to four years, through which the roots can grow to become very large. *Maintain*: hoe regularly and water in the summer. *Harvest*: dig out the roots between October and March. You can wrap the roots in kitchen paper and *store* for a few days in the vegetable tray of the refrigerator.

Cardamine: Cardamine has a strong, peppery flavor and can be eaten raw or as part of a salad. Unfortunately, this is not the sort of vegetable that you commonly find in the supermarket, so it's certainly worth the effort of growing it yourself. The plant requires a moisture retaining soil that is not over composted and a place in the sun or half-shade. In the ground the plant has a bitter taste, but once it blooms, the

flavor of the leaf becomes much more appealing. You can harvest the young leaf but make sure that you do not slice through the end of the root as this will kill the plant. *Sow* in July and August in order to harvest in the autumn or in March and June in order to be able to pick cardamine in the summer. Sow the seeds at a depth of 1 to 2 in or 2.5 to 5 cm, in rows with a mutual distance of 6 to 7 in or 15 to 18 cm. *Maintenance*: be aware of the ragwort flea beetle, especially at the start of the growth process. *Harvesting* can be done eight weeks from sowing. *Pick* the outer leaves of young plants and the hearts of the older vegetables. After the first year you won't to have to sow any new plants: a number of plants will remain and multiply. You will then only have to plant seedlings in a new spot.

Parsley root: Parsley is a type of vegetable of which you can eat both the leaf and the root. Parsley root is 6 to 8 in or 15 to 20 cm long. The vegetable is very popular in Germany, Hungary, Austria and Russia, where it's generally eaten as vegetable, but it's also used often in soups and stews. The parsley root has the deep, sweet flavor characteristic of dishes from those countries. You can *sow* it in April and May, but be sure to loosen the soil well beforehand. *Maintenance*: water regularly to keep the soil moist. It may take three to four weeks for the seeds to germinate. *Harvest* from the end of September.

Celeriac: This vegetable requires a gentle, moist climate and prefers a richly fertilized soil. Enrich the soil in the autumn with well-decomposed manure or composet without straw. Wait four years before sowing in the same place. Add a soluble fertilizer each month. *Sowing*: from February to April in a greenhouse. Plant the seedlings into nursery spaces once they have four or five leaves. Plant them out in the first two weeks of June in their definite spot. Keep a distance between plants of 14 in or 35 cm. *Maintenance*: Hoe regularly. Water at the foot of the plants. Remove any yellow leaves. *Harvest* before it turns cold in October and November. Celeriac can be kept in a cool, dry place. Do not wash it, but *store* it in sand.

Other vegetables this season: **parsnip, lambs' lettuce, spinach, chicory, red cabbage**.

B. The orchard

Spring

Strawberries: Strawberries are grown in almost every garden in the main section. Make sure that the soil has enough compost and fertilize with well-decomposed farmyard manure. Watch out for places with a late frost. The roots can reach up to 1 meter under the soil and do not grow horizontally below the surface. Fertilize the ground to a sufficient depth. The ideal time to plant them is at the end of July or the start of August. If you plant later than this, your harvest will be halved during the following year. In other words: the earlier you plant, the richer the harvest. Plant the annuals at a distance of 16 to 20 in or 40 to 50 cm from each other. Water before and after planting, when the blossom buds are forming in September-October and from the start of flowering to harvesting, from the end of May to mid-July. Immediately after harvesting, loosen the soil

and remove any weeds. Suitable types for the garden include: elvira, korona, florika, polka, senga sengana, elsanta, tenira, mieze schindler and ostara.

Summer

All types of berries:
Blueberry: Blue-black in color, originally from North America but grown in Europe since the 1950s. The blueberry grows in bunches on very high bushes.
Bilberry: small, matt-blue berries with deep purple flesh and juice with a sweet flavor. Originally from North America. Currant: Originally from Europe and West Asia, there are red and white varieties as well as a sweeter variety and a black variety. The bush can grow in half-shade or full sun. Currants are best planted in the autumn or as soon as possible in the spring. Enrich the soil every spring with compost. Strong red types: rote vierländer, rondom, rotet, rolan. Good white currants: versaillaise blanche. Suitable black currants: silvergieters black and titiana.
Blackberry: Black in color with a very unique, strong flavor.
Gooseberry: This type of berry can be green, yellow or red and has a sweet-sour flavor. Originally from Western and Central-Europe, these should be planted the same way as currants. They can be harvested from mid-May for a green crop and from July for the fully ripe berries. Recommended types of gooseberry: hinnonmäki, hönings früheste and rote triumph.

Peaches: If the tree stands protected next to a wall, for example on the south side, you will be able to grown peaches in a climate like that of Belgium, but you should know that the blossom will freeze during a heavy winter and the tree may not fruit in that year. Recommended types: rekord aus alfter, revita, benedicte and kernechter vom vorgebirge.

Wild strawberries: These grow across almost all of Belgium, particularly near trees in the half-shade. The fruit, really a false fruit, gives off a sweet scent and is edible. Just like the regular strawberry, wild strawberries have runners from which young plants grow. You can remove these and plant them. You can also sow the seeds. Harvest the fruit from around the end of June and July.

Cherries: This type of fruit has become increasingly more expensive due to the high costs of harvesting and is worth growing yourself for that reason alone. It is however the type that requires quite a lot of space (between 65 and 85 yd^2 or 60 and 80 m^2) and requires specific soil criteria. Moreover, it takes quite a lot of work to protect the crown against blackbirds and starlings, which love cherries. The cherry tree does not require so very much in the way of soil quality, only that it be sufficiently deep and potassium-rich and have a layer of compost. Cold, heavy soil should be avoided. Harvesting early types may start in June,

186

later types in July. Recommended types: kassins frühe, burlat, dönissens gelbe knorpelkirsche, bigarreau noir.

Autumn

Apples: You can eat apples from your own garden from the end of July to long into the springtime. Their diversity is amazing. Apple trees can be planted in even the smallest of gardens. The huge choice of rootstocks means you can match the size of the crown to the available space. Ideally use a nutrient-rich, loamy soil that is well ventilated and has a good layer of compost. If the soil does not meet these criteria, you can help this by adding fertilizer (for extra oxygen) and compost (for extra humus). These are just some of the possible types of apple tree for the garden: cox's orange (harvest October-January), boskoop (mid-October) and gloster (harvest mid-end October).

Pears: Most types of pear do not last as long as apples. Therefore, plant half as many pear trees as apple trees or even a third as many. If you do not eat the pears immediately or shortly after picking them, you can keep them by canning or preserving for winter. The pear tree requires more heat that an apple tree and prefers to be planted in a light, sandy loam.

Wild strawberries: see Summer.

C. The herb garden

The lovely thing about an herb garden is that you can plant your favorite herbs as part of a small garden or in a pot on a terrace. Most herbs don't take up much space and they also make lovely decorations. Generally one or two of each plant will be sufficient.

Basil: This herb requires a sunny, warm climate as well as nutritious, well-drained soil. *Sow* in April-May in the greenhouse. Plant the seedlings out in May-June or buy plants in May and put them in the garden. Maintain a distance of 25 cm between the plants and water them two or three times per week in dry weather. *Harvest* from June to October. You can *store* basil by drying the stems in a warm, dry place with the top of the sprig hanging downwards, and wrapped loosely in brown paper.

Chives: Chives are delicious in salads and with certain fish dishes. This herb requires lots of light, moist but well drained soil. *Sow* liberally from March to June and thin the seedlings out to a distance of 4 in or 10 cm or plant purchased plants. Maintain the plants by removing flowers as soon as they appear. *Harvest* from March to November, as close to the ground as possible. You can *store* them in the freezer in an airtight container.

Lemon balm: This serrated plant has a delicate lemony taste. It does well in fertile soil in slight shade in a wind-free spot. *Sow* in March and April in a greenhouse and then plant in the full soil. They're a prolific plant, so prune them in summer. *Harvest* just before the flowering season in May-June and in September. Leave the leaves to dry in a dry, well-ventilated spot.

Dill: This herb is delicious with fish. It prefers slightly dry, rocky ground, preferably in the sun. *Sow* in April-May, thin out the seedlings to a distance of 16 in or 40 cm. Maintain the plants with regular mounding. Pick as required. *Store* in a plastic bag in the refrigerator or hang up to dry in a warm place with the head of the sprig hanging downwards.

Tarragon: This plant enjoys light, permeable soil and prefers to be in slight shade. You cannot *sow* tarragon, but you can grow it in the springtime. As soon as the plant catches on, prune the ends of the stems in order to force them to make branches. *Maintain* them through the winter by pruning the stems and covering the plant with a layer of straw. Tarragon is best used fresh, as the taste is lost through drying. It's also delicious in vinegar or oil.

Chervil: Chervil is lovely in salads. The plant likes strong, nutritious soil, regular watering and a shady position. *Sow* from March to September 4 in or 10 cm apart. Do not thin out. Be sure to

water it every now and then. *Harvest* as desired. Cut flat above the ground. *Save* the fresh herbs in the refrigerator, wrapped in kitchen paper, or hang in dry space, loosely covered in brown paper.

Cilantro: This plant grows to be 24 in or 60 cm tall and flowers in the summer. Cilantro requires a warm or moderate climate, lots of sun and light soil, preferably containing calcium. *Sow* in April-May or in September. Place two to three seeds in holes 8 in or 20 cm apart, in rows 12 in or 30 cm apart. Keep only the best plants. All you need to do then is to hoe every now and then. *Harvest* from June. You can *keep* the herb for about a week in a plastic bag in the refrigerator.

Bay leaf: This bush likes to be in light, dry and well ventilated soil and does not do well at temperatures lower than 14 °F / -10 °C. The herb is slow to grow from seed and you would do best to buy some plants in the springtime or plant in September. *Prune* at the start of the autumn. Pick the leaves throughout the entire year, as desired. To *store*, place the bay leaves in an air-tight box away from the light.

Mint: Green mint is the most common type grown in gardens. It can reach 18 in or 45 cm in height. The plant likes compost rich and moist, even heavy types of soil and to be planted in half-shade. Sowing is difficult. It's better to buy two or three plants and plant them from March to May, 8 to 12 in or 20 to 30 cm apart. Best to plant mint in a pot to prevent the plants from proliferating. *Harvest* on a dry day. *Store* the leaves in a well-ventilated, dry place.

Parsley: Parsley grows well in a moderate climate and prefers loose and compost rich soil. Sow in February to March and thin the seedlings to a distance of 4 to 6 in or 10 to 15 cm. Make 2 in or 5 cm deep wells and place the seed into these. Cover with a layer of compost and press down on the soil. Water the plants regularly. Cut off the leaves, but do not damage the young shoots in the centre of the plant. *Save* in the vegetable tray in the refrigerator, freeze or hang up to dry with the head of the bunch downwards.

Rosemary: This bushy pant does well in potassium-rich soil and does not like too much moisture. In April-May plant two or three purchased plants and place them about 19.5 in or 50 cm apart. Water the plants, but not too much. Harvest as desired. *Save* by drying or freezing bunches of the plant.

Sage: This herb is delicious with red meat, poultry and fish. The plant is not demanding. You can plant sage in the ground or in ceramic pots with a diameter of 7 to 8 or 18 to 20 cm, filled three quarters full with compost and one-third with sand. You can *sow* in the springtime; it will be ready in the autumn when you should remove any sprigs that look bad. Refresh the plants every five years. Allow the leaves to dry flat in the dark.

Thyme: This little plant needs sun year round. Germination takes two to three weeks. Plant out in April-May or in September. Prune in the springtime, removing half of the plants to encourage new shoots. Only pick the green parts of the stems and not the bottom half of the plant. To dry, hang the sprigs up for three weeks in bunches with tops down.

ACKNOWLEDGEMENTS

I would like first and foremost to thank my team. The ladies and gentlemen who do their absolute best to make the best of a business like Elckerlijc and to always make our guests as comfortable as possible. Thanks go to Tom van den Broeck for thinking about the presentation of the dishes in this book.

USEFUL LINKS

› www.outdoorchef.com
› www.dutry.be
› www.lepanyol.com
› www.matro.com
› www.grill-dome.nl
› www.kitchenaid.be
› www.bon-fire.dk
› www.weber.com
› www.boretti.nl
› www.elckerlijc.be
› www.deolijfboom.be (herbs and spices)
› www.comptoir-des-epices.eu (herbs and spices)
› www.cnudde.com (smoking gun, truffle caviar)
› www.ghecom.be (smoke generator and herbs Peter De Clercq, Point-Virgule)
› www.drinkiq.com

WWW.LANNOO.COM

Register on our website and we will regularly
send you a newsletter with information about
new books and interesting, exclusive offers.

Restaurant Elckerlijc
Kraailokerkweg 17
9990 Maldegem
Belgium
T + 32 (0) 50 71 52 63
F + 32 (0) 50 71 47 22
www.elckerlijc.be – info@elckerlijc.be

Recipes:	Peter De Clercq
Text:	Sofie Vanherpe
Photography:	Lennert Deprettere
Design:	Studio Lannoo
Lay-out and translation:	Textcase

If you have observations or questions,
please contact our editorial office:
redactielifestyle@lannoo.com

© Lannoo Publishers, Tielt, Belgium, 2012
D/2012/45/292 – NUR 440
ISBN: 978-94-014-0255-2